Happy Birthday to another
"Extraordinary Woman"!
Love
Rose Margaret
Jan. 2002

Portraits of
Extraordinary Women

Portraits of Extraordinary Women

Text by William F. Maestri

Portraits by
Marilyn Carter Rougelot

Foreword by Sheila Bosworth

PELICAN PUBLISHING COMPANY

Gretna 1997

Special thanks to editor Ashley Ellington

*The word "Pelican" and the depiction of a pelican are trademarks
of Pelican Publishing Company, Inc., and are registered
in the U.S. Patent and Trademark Office.*

Library of Congress Cataloging-in-Publication Data

Maestri, William.
    Portraits of extraordinary women / text by William F. Maestri ; por-
traits by Marilyn Carter Rougelot ; foreword by Sheila Bosworth.
      p.   cm.
    ISBN 1-56554-242-8 (hc : alk. paper)
    1. Women in the Bible—Biography. 2. Bible—Biography. I.
Rougelot, Marilyn. II. Title.
    BS575.M32 1997
    220.9'22'082—dc21   96-53060
                                                     CIP

Printed in Hong Kong
Published by Pelican Publishing Company, Inc.
1101 Monroe Street, Gretna, Louisiana 70053

For our parents, Andrew and Melba Carter,
and Ferdinand and Elaine Maestri, who gave without measure
so that we might accept the challenge of life through the blessings of faith

Contents

Biblical Passages for Reference

1. Eve (Genesis 2:18-3:24)
2. Sarah and Hagar (Genesis Chapters 12-23)
3. Lot's Wife (Genesis 19:15-28)
4. Jezebel (1 Kings Chapters 16-21; Revelation 2:18-29)
5. Ruth and Naomi (Book of Ruth)
6. Delilah (Judges 13:1-25; Chapter 16)
7. Judith (Book of Judith, Chapters 8-16)
8. Bathsheba (2 Samuel, Chapters 11 and 12; 1 Kings Chapter 1 and 2)
9. Esther (Book of Esther)
10. Deborah (Judges Chapter 4:1-24; 5:1-31)
11. Tamar (Genesis Chapters 38 and 49)
12. Susanna (Greek Version, Chapter 13)
13. Elizabeth (Luke 1:5-25; 39-45; 56-66; 80)
14. Samaritan Woman at the Well (John 4:14-42)
15. Poor Widow (Luke 21:1-4)
16. Herodias and Salome (Mark 6:14-29)
17. Woman Caught in Adultery (John 8:1-11)
18. Woman with a Hemorrhage (Mark 5:21-43)
19. Martha and Mary (Luke 10:38-42; John 11:1-46)
20. Mother of James and John (Mark 10:35-45; Matthew 20:20-28)
21. Woman Who Anoints Jesus (Matthew 26:6-13; Luke 7:36-50; John 12:1-8)
22. Mary Magdalene (John 20:1-18; Matthew 27:54-56; Mark 16:9-11; Luke 24:10-11)
23. Priscilla (Acts of the Apostles 18:24-28)
24. Mary (Luke 1:26 -38, 46-55; John 1:1-18; 19:25-27)

Foreword

The English novelist E. M. Forster's famous dictum to those who seek to create art consists of two words: "Only connect." First of all, above all, "connect."

If art is defined as the use of things to answer some special purpose, as the employment of means to accomplish some end, then according to Forster, the end the artist strives to attain is nothing less than the creation of a meaningful and lasting bond between the work of art and humanity. A true work of art inspires in us a bittersweet jolt of recognition, a pleasurable shock of communal feeling, a sense of oneness with the rest of mankind. Art reassures us that we are not alone in our sorrow, our fear, our longing, our joy. If there is one universal human experience, it is that of pain, which mankind alone of God's creatures has the ability to recall and to anticipate. The work of art called *Portraits of Extraordinary Women* deals with the pain of being human—more specifically, of being woman—over and over again, not in order to discourage, but to console and inspire. "When pain is to be borne," wrote the Anglican theologian and novelist C. S. Lewis, "a little courage helps more than much knowledge, a little human sympathy more than much courage, and the least tincture of God's love more than all." *Portraits of Extraordinary Women* abounds in the courage, knowledge, and sympathy of the two artists who created it.

The painter Marilyn Carter Rougelot employs the brushstrokes of oil on canvas in the creation of her art.

Father William Maestri, the author of the text that accompanies Ms. Rougelot's portraits of women of the Old and New Testaments, uses language to connect with the hearts and minds of his readers.

The result is perhaps less collaboration than coalescence; it is a coming together of portrait and text, each of which works independently. But

11

when they are combined, they enrich one another immeasurably. With the certainty and courage of an artist's vision, Ms. Rougelot depicts these women exactly as their situations in life reveal them to be, in a light so bright with honesty that their images burn into our souls. Father Maestri, in the Old Testament tradition of rabbi as symbolist and moralist, adds to the painter's unblinking illumination of truth the hopeful shadings of his own vision of mankind, not simply as it was and is, but as it can be with the help of divine grace. There is that sense of inevitability to both portraits and text that marks all true art. The words that accompany each portrait are not interchangeable; they arise from an authentic understanding of the individual they describe and explain, and no other. The portraits, in turn, meet the standards of the French painter Jean-François Millet who wrote, "I try not to have things look as if chance brought them together, but as if they had a necessary bond between them. I want the people I represent to look as if they really belonged to their station, so that imagination cannot conceive of their ever being anything else."

Henry James noted that "it takes a lot of history to produce a little art." A history, of course, is a drama dealing with past events in the life of a community. The history that is the sacred text comprising the Old and New Testaments is the drama of the community of mankind from the moment of creation. It is this drama that is the subject of *Portraits of Extraordinary Women*, and it is in this aspect of the book as history that the idea of connecting takes on additional meaning. The women portrayed here have connected with humanity for three thousand years; in these women, for good or ill, we recognize ourselves. These females caught in the act—in acts of faith, hope, love, contrition, foolishness, folly, fear, and triumph—are powerful individuals, extraordinary creatures, though some are nameless. They are women who respond, who take risks, who right wrongs, and who provide for posterity negative as well as positive examples.

But in addition to their emotional connection with us, there is a chronological connection, the connection of cause and effect. Consider the portrait of Eve, arms outstretched to the tree of sin and death. Eve's grasp reaches down the centuries to the tree of the Cross of Christ, on which the Redeemer, true God and true Man, suffered crucifixion and death to restore humanity to eternal life. Contemplate the portrait of Ruth, the young widow at her widowed mother-in-law's side. There is devotion and determination in her foreigner's eyes; her strong-boned face is alight with her willingness to glean barley and wheat in Boaz's field beyond Bethlehem. Where is the historical connection to us here? Novelist and essayist Cynthia Ozick, in *Metaphor and Memory*, recalls a portrait of Ruth that hung in her house when she was a child, a portrait that was placed next to one of her grandfather, a Hebrew scholar whose life was spent almost wholly in a study filled with books. What is the connection, asks Ozick, between her grave, pale, intellectual ancestor and Ruth, young and vibrant, "the woman . . . standing barefoot" in the field? "Everything," comes Ozick's answer, "everything. She, the Moabite, is why he, when hope is embittered, murmurs the Psalms of David. The track her naked toes make in Boaz's field . . . is the very track his forefinger follows across the letter-speckled sacred page."

Only connect.

What is the connection between author and painter in a work such as this? Two such different gifts as writing and painting surely require different approaches to the task of producing a book.

Father William Maestri writes carefully, quickly, intensely, and by hand. His text is powered by a theologian's knowledge and understanding, a teacher's zeal, and a confessor's compassion. He completed the text at his own rapid pace, independent of Marilyn Carter Rougelot's paintings.

Ms. Rougelot's method was to first read the scriptural text applicable to each portrait, then to research *Dictionary of the Bible* by John L. McKenzie, S.J., for additional historical background. Next, she read Father Maestri's text, and finally, she slipped into a realm of the imagination, where she became present within the biblical scene she sought to render on canvas. Observing the drama from the sidelines, watching moments in the story, trusting her instincts, she catches the woman at the defining point in the action, and then transfers the woman and the moment from the inner canvas of her mind to the canvas on the easel. It is this process that gives us the singular, terrifying portrait of Lot's wife with fire in her eyes; of the widow, touchingly young and unexpectedly joyful in the giving of her mite to the Temple coffers; of Mary, the mother of Jesus, whose eyes in Ms. Rougelot's interpretation are not downcast but strong, intelligent, gazing straight ahead into her blessed and sorrowful role in the history of mankind. (In the single departure from the prose form of his other texts, Father Maestri accompanies this portrait of Mary with eloquent, elegant poetry.)

As different as their creative methods are, both author and painter were surely aware from its inception that a work such as this is a hazardous undertaking. It is, after all, a book intended for a wide, varied audience, male and female, old and young, Christian and non-Christian. It is a challenge to that audience as well as a consolation. It is no simple picture book designed solely to enhance the decor of the home library. And the women it depicts are icons, ancient historical figures that, beloved or notorious, are viewed in long-held, particular detail by each individual familiar with their stories. But in order to create art, writer and painter must dare to trust the God-given talent that impels the artist to put pen to paper and brush to canvas without regard to pleasing any particular faction among an audience. To take that chance is the artist's duty as well as privilege, but it's not easy to do. In *Last Tales*, by the Danish writer Isak Dinesen, a woman asks a storyteller, " 'Are you sure that it is God whom you serve?' The Cardinal looked up, met her eyes, and smiled very gently. 'That,' he said, 'that, Madame, is a risk which the artists and priests of the world have to run.' "

—SHEILA BOSWORTH

Portraits of
Extraordinary Women

Introduction:
Sketches on a Canvas

David is in the middle course of life. There is a gnawing restlessness which bespeaks a not so quiet desperation. It is not the mid-life crisis of pop psychology or the psycho-babble of daytime talk TV. It is a hunger for deep down things, which the cornucopia of the modern mall cannot satisfy.

Enough's enough.

David has traded in the BMW for a tractor. The gray canyons of Wall Street have been left for the big sky of Montana. Power lunches and closing-the-deal dinners, with glad hands and plastic smiles, have been replaced with the noon meal and supper. Bread is now broken with those once strangers in the house who have become family.

Cybil, of the forty-something generation, has come of age in a time of liberation. She has shattered the glass ceiling and risen the corporate ladder. All the perks are hers: key to the executive bathroom; private parking space; and a secretary (a male!) to make the coffee. Yet Cybil is running on empty. The high-rise apartment is a white sepulcher, filled with the trophies of success but lacking in loving arms to receive *her*. The martini is dry and the dinner for one is low fat. In between reading the latest quarterly report and viewing a video, Cybil does her best to suppress the old *ennui*. The winged chariot of time sounds its own alarm. Cybil continues to play dodge-ball with those troubling twins: Why? and How Long? For now, one more chablis as the VCR fades to black. Tomorrow's another day, Cybil.

Although we have not met David and Cybil, we know them. They populate our lives and stare back at us in the morning mirror. We experience the weight of Sisyphus's rock. The morning after the day before has a dull, numbing sameness. Our resolve is tested to keep on keeping on. The

17

modern promise of happiness through material progress has not material-
ized. The soul goes unnourished. The spirit does not soar. We do not live
without bread; but by bread alone we do not flourish.

There is a nineties version of the sixties' dropping out and turning on.
The current spin does not come by way of drugs, free sex, and the angry
exhibitionism of the materially pampered. Today's counter-culture gospel
is preached, not by hippies with beads and braids, but by a generation of
seekers. The Age of Aquarius has matured into a middle age, struggling
with the middle course of life. The time of achievement in the fast lane is
now the time of reassessment along those off-track paths of family, community, and spirituality. It is not a time of flight from the world as much
as a time of looking at old goals with new eyes. The tectonic plates of success and the good life have been shifting. A fault line has been opened to
include the things of the spirit.

Seekers need guides to show the way. Companions for the journey can
stride across the ages and transcend the barriers of culture, race, age, religion, and gender. A common quest melts the differences and brings to
light our shared humanity. Beneath the external strangeness there is a
common wisdom which finds a home in the restless heart.

The Bible contains numerous portraits of fellow seekers who can serve
as guides. In the midst of our present search for meaning, women in the
Scriptures extend a hand. One need not be a believer. No litmus test of
orthodoxy or political correctness is required. To grasp the hand of these
wise women requires but a willingness to be open to all things human, for
it is in the wonder of the human that we encounter the divine. It is in the
fragility of the flesh that the spirit soars. We never travel so near to God
as when we journey into our humanity. And these biblical women, revealed in portrait and text, come through the ages to refresh.

All is here to ponder: courage and cowardice; grace and sin; hope and
despair; failure and the power to begin anew. Above all we find an enduring truth about that invincible spring in which life rises through the white
blanket of winter. Whether the sun is just rising on our day, or the shadows are lengthening on our brief span of time, life goes on. The monuments of our worth are forever cast in those off-camera moments of everyday kindness, heroism, generosity, failure, forgiveness, courage, and hope.
It is in the marrow of the ordinary that extraordinary truth is revealed.

A word of clarification must be offered. Biblical women encompass the
complexity and truth of the human condition. There is the moral courage
of Susanna as well as the weakness of Bathsheba. The majesty of Esther is
balanced by the poverty of the poor widow. The virtue of Ruth as well as
the vice of Delilah is acknowledged. Some of our women do not have
names; they are instead identified by their status or condition. Women

without names ought not surprise us—it is a common method of trivializing their status.

   The women selected for our gallery of portraits do not come free of folly. They are not too good to be true. Rather, these women illustrate the rich texture of our humanity. And the canvas on which they are painted must reveal our capacity for sin, banality, and vindictiveness, as well as heroism and sacrifice. There is wisdom in knowing what to avoid and whom to shun, as well as knowing what to do and whom to befriend. We who have painted and written what follows are seekers. This labor of paint and print has enriched us in ways beyond measure. To whom much is given, much is expected. Hence, we offer this book in gratitude to our fellow seekers of another time who are now our guides. We offer this book to our fellow seekers of today, with the humble hope that together we will find that truth which sets us free.

> And in the last days it shall be, God declares,
> that I will pour out my Spirit upon all flesh,
> and your sons and your daughters shall prophesy,
> and your young men shall see visions,
> and your old men shall dream dreams;
> yea, and on my menservants and my maidser-
>   vants in those days
> I will pour out my Spirit; and they shall
>   prophesy.
> And I will show wonders in the heaven above
>   and signs on the earth beneath
>   —Joel 2:28-29

1

Eve:
Know Your Limits

Like the classic movie we've seen time and again, we look at Eve about to reach for the forbidden fruit which exceeds her grasp. We want to yell, "Don't do it!" Yet she does. And here *we* are.

We are the "poor banished children of Eve" living our own version of reach exceeding grasp. Yet we add, with a residue of that first rebellion, "but isn't that what a heaven is for?"

Modern pop psychology praises the adventurous, autonomous self which tests limits and exceeds boundaries. We are assured that the healthy personality is one which takes risks and explores the world. To such individuals our therapeutic culture bestows its praise; the chorus proclaims "high self-esteem." Hence it is deemed a sign of dysfunction to acknowledge limits and respect boundaries. We are often told that those who hang No Trespassing signs are fearful authorities simply marking their turf and holding on to their privilege.

However, here is God commanding (not suggesting), "You may freely eat of every tree of the garden; but of the tree of knowledge of good and evil you shall not eat, for in the day that you eat of it you shall die" (Gen 2:16-17). The mere fact that God commands, and sets limits on our freedom, makes the forbidden more attractive and the ego more determined to possess. And if we need encouragement to fuel our pride, the Tempter provides a fine mixture of doubt and distrust.

"Did God say, 'You shall not eat of any tree of the garden'?" The work of the Serpent begins with a question that is really an incitement—God sets limits which are contrary to life and reason. Eve corrects the Serpent but the damage has been done. For she adds her own distortion to the limits set by God: "neither shall you *touch* it." The Serpent now knows she's hooked, for truth and trust have been undermined by exaggeration. Can the big lie be far behind? Hardly.

"But the Serpent said to the woman, 'You shall not die. For God knows that when you eat of it your eyes will be opened, and you will be like God, knowing good and evil.' "

The tangled web of deception and doubt draws its prey tight as the bonds of trust between God and Eve begin to unravel. What begins in the mind as doubt quickly races to excite the senses and give a rush to the passions. The forbidden now becomes a delight to the eyes and the source of wisdom. There before her, dangling, is the trophy that is to be consumed. But the prize must be shared. Adam, strangely silent, is drawn into the quest for divinity; we need companions for our folly. Sin is seldom cloistered. There is no such thing as a little pride.

It is consummated: "Then their eyes were opened and they knew that they were naked; and they sewed fig leaves together and made themselves aprons." Their pride becomes their shame. The tree on which hung their hopes must now provide a cover for their despair. Their opened eyes provide the knowledge without innocence. The dash is on to blame: God, the Tempter, the Other. The usual suspects. The rest is history, as they say, East of Eden with its pain of banishment.

This is the way it was, but God's love refuses to let it always be so. East of Eden will unfold that *love* yet untold, but in the fullness of time became visible in the Word made flesh. The proud reached up in order to look down on everyone. Yet with God it is the opposite. God reached down in Jesus so that we might be lifted up and healed. The Serpent comes to tempt at our strongest moments so that we fall in pride. Jesus comes at our weakest moments so that we might rise.

Other traditions have their stories of pride, fall, and punishment: Icarus flies too high and close to the sun; Prometheus and Sisyphus suffer for their hubris; and Faust must pay the devil. However, it is with the Christian story that God acts on our behalf. And what an act it is: God empties himself in Jesus and becomes one with our humanity in humility. The tree that once held the symbol of disobedient pride now lifts up the Suffering Servant who turns our death to life and banishment to welcome home.

A difficult lesson to learn is this: love places limits and freedom matures with boundaries. Good parents dare to incur the short-term displeasure of their children by setting limits. Be home at midnight. Stay in the front yard. Call when you arrive at the party. Such "fun-killing" injunctions and boundaries to freedom mark one as "mean," "not trusting," or "forgetful of once being young." To be sure, parental resolve can dissolve under the acids of "everybody's doing it" or "all the cool people will be there." Wise parents don't argue. They hold firm. And in time the children of their children become schooled in that same love which sets limits. Parents hear the echoes of their love in the voices of their children who now parent a new generation. So it goes.

Boundless freedom is really chaos. Lack of commitment is a sign of immaturity. Liberty becomes license. In a culture which sings "My Way" as its theme song, boundaries are viewed as blockades to self-realization, fulfillment, and just plain self-indulgence. Marriage is a trap. Contracts are made to be broken. Friendship is as solid as Jell-O. The conventional wisdom you know.

Yet we are never so free as when we pledge ourselves in donation to that person or cause beyond the self and the tyranny of the moment. Only the free can say, "until death do us part," "I promise," "you can count on me."

Such is the way of God with us: a love that dares the supreme commitment in Bethlehem and pays the ultimate price on Calvary. For in Jesus total love and true freedom unite. Crib and Cross are one. We poor children of Eve no longer feel the need to be like God. Because of Jesus we can accept our humanity, and not be ashamed. We no longer mourn for that Paradise Lost. Our banishment had led to that Kingdom "of the poor in spirit," formed by the One "who is meek and humble of heart." There, and in Him, we find rest for our souls.

2

Sarah and Hagar:
A Tale of Two Women

At the heart of drama is conflict: the irresistible force and the immovable object. But in the Bible the drama comes by way of strong characters more than forces and objects: God and Job; Moses speaking truth to the power of Pharaoh; Jesus revealing the weakness of Pilate; and the Apostle Paul confronting the foolishness of the Galatians, to name but a few.

Strong characters provide high drama and quality conflict. Two such characters are Sarah and Hagar. Each in her own way is a woman of strength. The conflict is in the contrast.

Sarah is up in years but retains that beauty which time enhances. She is a woman of substance, and is well connected through a sound marriage. Sarah is "liberated" but infertile. And this barrenness is her flaw. There is a hardness about Sarah which comes from being without child. It is seen through her beauty. Her face is etched with a kind of weathered look and toughness, brought on by the drying rays of glances and nods from "well-meaning friends." To be childless is a reproach, not an option. Sarah's eyes reflect a deep truth: the more one is blessed, the more painful the Cross; the more striking the beauty, the more pronounced the flaw.

Even her laughter at the news of deliverance is wrapped in the shell of skepticism. Sarah will not be fooled or hurt again. No more empty promises, promises. No more hope against hope. This is Sarah the wise. She knows the score and can read the calendar. The years have had their way.

Hagar is young and possesses that beauty which turns heads and excites passions. She is a woman in bondage, but she is fertile. And her fertility is the source of her anguish as well as her hope. For if Sarah cannot choose her infertility, neither can Hagar choose with whom she will be intimate.

Hagar's beauty is that of youth, but it carries the aging of her status. It

25

is a beauty chiseled in the granite face of a slave girl. Smoldering beneath the beauty is a fire flamed by others' demands and needs. There is a danger in Hagar that men sense and women know.

The poor do the bidding of the rich. Sarah cannot conceive.

Hagar can.

Will.

Does.

The gender bond between Sarah and Hagar is non-existent. Worlds collide. Sarah, Pharaoh-like, will visit her years of resentment on Hagar. There is no tender mercy. Hagar, like Israel, flees into the desert. Yet there is no offer of a Promised Land. She must return to Sarah and "submit."

Why? How can the God of Liberation renew the oppression?

These questions which tumble from the modern sensibilities will not be easily satisfied with the ways of God. Yet here it is: if Hagar does not return she will surely die. She will no longer enjoy the "protection" of her mistress. In flight, her vulnerability grows. These are the facts, ma'am, just the facts. Those on the margins seldom possess options. There are few ways out of life's traps.

There is also an insight into God's ways. Namely, God works within the givens of the tangled web of complex relationships we humans weave. Heart and history are complex. There are no microwave answers prepared at the touch of a button. Fast foods do not nourish. Quick answers do not satisfy. God must touch the hearts of stone with a patient grace that yields a heart of flesh. Hence, Hagar will return and submit. Hagar will give birth to Ishmael. And more, God will multiply her offspring. Those in dire straits are not abandoned by the Lord.

God has only just begun. He must work on Sarah. And her make-over calls for a change of name and that grace which brings forth life in the most barren of situations. True to his word, the Sarai of skeptical laughter has now become Sarah of a joyful laugh. Her reproach has ended. Abraham will have *that* son of *that* covenant through whom the world will receive its Savior!

Yet a change in name, and a promise kept, are not enough to overcome the years with their memories of a womb that never bore and breasts that never nursed. A narrowness of vision, and a sclerosis of the heart, will not allow Sarah to see Hagar as anything but a slave and Ishmael as anything but a rival to Isaac. Slave and rival must be "cast out." Sarah will finally be relieved of her discontent. Once again Abraham is being asked to sacrifice what is dear: he is to place bread, water, and son on the shoulder of Hagar. The wilderness awaits to receive its wanderers.

Where is God to be found?

Do promises to Sarah count for more than those to Hagar?

Resources are depleted. Ishmael's life, and God's word, hang in the balance. Again, where is the Lord to be found?

When human limits are reached, God is most present. What is lacking in us is made up by the God who hears the cries of the poor. At the broken places, God's healing grace is at work. In our weakness God is strong for us. Hagar and Ishmael will not be abandoned. God sees and provides. The poor are not invisible to the Lord. Sarah has cast out Hagar, but in the wilderness God's angel says "come" and be restored to life. Hagar and Ishmael were never out of God's sight; their cries never beyond the hearing of an ear connected to the heart.

At the end we return to the beginning. We are once again with Sarah and Hagar. Their drama is ours. We too struggle to reconcile our differences, to experience that healing which would allow the children of Sarah to play with the children of Hagar.

Yet the outcasts are still with us. The urban wilderness continues to collect those who fall through the safety net of our social concern, the enslaved of the world where cries reach no ear and where plight is out of sight.

Where is the Lord to be found?

The God of the wilderness is the Lord of our modern deserts. God still works within the givens of history to change hearts. The God who spoke promises to Abraham, Sarah, and Hagar speaks today to those without hope. The God who hears the cries of Ishmael listens to the weeping of today's children. God continues to open eyes to the wells of living water in the most arid of places.

God still sends his messengers among us with words of courage: "Do not be afraid . . . I am your shield."

3

Lot's Wife:
Looking Back

There are figures in literature, sacred and secular, which endure because of the insights they reveal about the human condition. One such figure is Lot's wife, whose brief story is told in Genesis (19:15-26). This unnamed woman (how predictable!) is turned into a pillar of salt because she violated the Lord's command "not to look back." She is often held up as an example of the fate that awaits those who disobey, hesitate, or become fascinated with evil. In the Gospel of Luke, Jesus warns his audience that even the most pressing demands of friends and family cannot come before the Kingdom. For those who turn back, the fate of Lot's wife awaits them (17:32).

The great theologian of the early Greek-speaking church, Origen (184-254 A.D.), preached a homily entitled "On Lot and His Daughters." The fate of Lot's wife is a reminder of sin's power to fascinate and attract, even for those in flight by God's command. Why? Because sin appeals to the eye and feels good to the flesh. Origen holds her up as representing the flesh (Lot represents "the rational understanding and manly soul"). And "it is the flesh which always looks to vices, which, when the soul is proceeding to salvation, looks backward and seeks after pleasure." Lot's wife is viewed by Origen as the embodiment of folly. She is turned into a pillar of salt which is symbolic of prudence, the virtue she lacks. Lot's wife doesn't know when to cut losses and get out while she can. How like us! One more for the road. One last cut of the deck or toss of the dice. What can it hurt?

Often Scripture's greatest revelations of truth about God and his wonderfully made and perplexing creatures come in seemingly minor episodes. So it is with Lot's wife. There is a command, a response, and a consequence. So simple. Yet there is more here than just a spiritual appetizer.

29

We are not simply being given an example of Old Testament "tough love." Rather, an important course in human development is being served.

God does not beat around the burning bush. What is required is direct: "Flee for your life; do not look back." The Lord is going to destroy Sodom and Gomorrah because of the pervasiveness of sin (lust and inhospitality). Mercy has run its course. Abraham had petitioned for clemency. God relented. The situation grew worse. God's compassion has been perverted into a sign of weakness. Now the Lord must act. There comes a time when evil must be confronted and overcome; neglect is not benign. From Sodom and Gomorrah, to Nazi Germany, to the urban centers of violent neglect, evil must be exorcised. To say nothing, to do nothing, is that cowardice masquerading as caution which values security more than truth.

Human evil can become so great that only the Divine can right the wrong. Even God's chosen ones must flee from both the evil and the wrath. Time is at a premium—flee now! Evil is so attractive and appealing to the heart that looking back is but a step to going back.

Evil brings on an anxiety attack which shortens the breath, moistens the palms, dries the mouth, and knots the stomach. Evil bedevils the imagination and weakens the will with the poison of self-doubt: "you will return; you can never be free;" so goes its enslaving refrain. For to flee and not look back is to risk pilgrimage into an unknown future. Old demons are better than new ones. We make friends with our devils and become comfortable with our vices. Better the land of slavery and three squares, than to venture into the Promised Land of yet-to-be-tasted milk and honey.

The Lord knows how attracted we are to that evil which dresses itself in the garb of a familiar friend. We must *both* flee *and* not look back. To flee but look back is to hold on to the past that determines the present and forecloses the future. Lot's wife cannot make that clean break which conquers each addiction. There remains a fascination with the forbidden. The residue of the Fall continues in the heart and whispers of what appears to be a "lost good." The eye is the window to the soul. And in the eye of Lot's wife there is reflected her longing for what she can no longer have. Such is known by all who must battle the bottle and break the grip of that white devil dust.

Honesty requires that we acknowledge our kinship with Lot's wife. In our more candid moments we find her human, sympathetic, and all too familiar. She is like a distant mirror which reflects our image. We slink away from the dessert tray as our resolve grows weaker with each backward glance. We know the magnetic pull exerted by that first summer love and its splendor in the grass. Its mystic magic grows as our autumn loves lengthen into winter. We never quite get out of our system that expensive toy, car, or dress. We buy what is more sensible, but our craving for the extravagant abides. We look at the car wreck through spaced fingers over the eyes. Carnage fascinates and repels. We look back to be reassured of our good fortune as we give voice to our sorrow for the victims.

We too live with divided eyes: one backward and one forward. Like an anxious figure in a Hitchcock thriller, we drive forward with eyes fixed on the rearview mirror. Our present is judged on the basis of what might have been. We mourn for that road not taken; that opportunity not seized; that victory not realized. There is a subliminal tape, a background refrain in the canyons of our imagination, which repeats, "if only."

The salting of Lot's wife does not take place in an instant. Her looking back on that day of flight bespeaks a life of living over the shoulder.

Sodom is her Eden. She looks with a melancholy longing for that Paradise Lost by a reach which exceeded a humble grasp.

Gomorrah is her Garden. The return to Eden is blocked by the cherubim with flaming swords. The return to Gomorrah is prevented by a consuming flame of divine wrath.

So it is with us. We banished children of Eve, and kin of Lot's wife, live in the mode of rewind. The past is our present and future. Our eye reflects that longing to go home again. We look backward for the mythic place of peace and joy. Slowly we turn into that tombstone of salt—brittle and bitter.

Yet there is also a look which is not a melancholy longing. There is the gaze of faith, a window to the soul, which bespeaks a saving grace. The eye does not contain those flames of destruction, but that fire of the Spirit which makes all things new. We consider not the things of the past. We look forward in hope to the best which is yet to be.

Also there is a salt which flavors and brings zest to life; a salt praised by Jesus as symbolic of the true disciple. This salt is born of that prudent courage which refuses to look back in anger, or flee into the future in order to forget. The salt that spices accepts the past as past and dares to move forward. That self-recrimination which gives rise to self-pity is not indulged. The spider's web of some sinful past does not trap its prey. But the resolute heart breaks those silky strands of yesterday, so that today can be lived as a gift, and tomorrow anticipated with hope.

4

Jezebel:
Fatal Attraction

The folly of those in high places is the belief that they are exempt from the laws of human nature, that money, power, and position entitles one to a free ride through life. Those obligations and influences that affect mere mortals are not for them.

A case in point, with a timeless and timely ring, is Ahab, the king of Israel. He foolishly believes that the power of his position protects him from God's judgment. The Lord's anointed can do as he pleases without consequence.

His prideful arrogance is magnified when he takes Jezebel, the pagan Phoenician, as his wife. Again he claims to be above the influence of intimate relationships. The whispers and favors of his wife, lurking behind the royal throne and inner chamber, carry no weight. Yet this fatal attraction will be his downfall. Ahab and Jezebel, king and queen, are public figures in high places—unfortunately for low purposes.

The political pundits that surrounded Ahab termed the marriage "good politics." What better way to turn a rival into an ally than by tying the knot? This contract of convenience secures the borders and establishes domestic tranquillity. Again, the folly of arrogance: the politically expedient is too often secured at the expense of religious integrity. Ahab cannot render to the realm of politics what ultimately belongs to the Lord of all realms. It is the tearing asunder of morality and politics; public life indifferent to faith secures not the borders and undermines the soul of the nation. The serving of many gods leads to disaster. Idolatry leads to the loss of peace at home and abroad. Destruction and death follow. Moral rot at the top works its way through the body politic. With a loss of spiritual insight, the entire nation falls blindly into a ditch.

Ahab soon learns that Jezebel does not subscribe to the separation of religion from the royal life. She is a queen who expects her gods to reign as well. Jezebel is a true believer. So is Elijah. He is "the prophet of the small voice" whose message is loud: there is only room for Yahweh. Jezebel's intent is clear: the blood of the prophets must run. Israel will once again be consecrated in the crucible of truth. And so the blood flows.

The lofty on mighty thrones view life in terms of grand designs. Details are often irritants to be handled by underlings. Yet the devil is in the details, as every lawyer knows. The fine print, the dotted *is* and crossed *ts*, is the hinge on which large events and lasting commitments swing. Small stones derail big trains. Promising projects go unfinished for want of a nail or penny.

The influence of intimate relationships, spouse or confidant, cannot be cloistered in rules or roles. There is an ebb and flow of human ties which penetrates the public and the private. There is no private indiscretion which does not weaken public integrity. Private vice works against public virtue. The stage of moral integrity encompasses both home and office; palace and retreat house; school and study; power lunch and shareholders' meeting. The "small" and secret sins of the inner chamber, in time, are shouted from the rooftops.

Jezebel teaches Ahab a painful lesson ever old and ever new: fatal attractions often have their genesis in seemingly innocent gestures and intimate relationships.

No one will be hurt. We're all consenting adults. Let's keep religion and morality out of this. Those at the top know best; just trust. Rationalizations all, yet they continue to beguile.

Ahab's Jezebel drops off the biblical screen, only to reappear in the book of Revelation *within* the church at Thyatira. The historical Jezebel has become an enduring symbol of that folly which asserts that we can flirt with evil and not be contaminated.

Church members at Thyatira are numbered within the ranks of the well-to-do. There is a great deal of pressure to go along in order to get along. You know: it makes good business sense to fit in. Money, commerce, and the marketplace require a "reasonable" attitude. One can be immersed in mammon (those possessions we love in place of God) and follow the trends without risk to faith. It's Economics 101.

The Jezebel of Thyatira is preaching that one can do business as usual, sample everyone's religion, and taste an eclectic morsel of morality without consequence for the inner person. This Jezebel separates the outer from the inner. Attitude and intention are primary, says our latest Jezebel. Conduct and behavior are mere externals; they count for naught. Inner purity and nobility of intention trump the requirements of moral action. Have a good intention, pure and noble, and do what you will. This is a perversion of Saint Augustine's love and do what you will.

The angel sent to the church of Thyatira labels the teachings of Jezebel "immoral." This label seems to libel, especially to sensitive ears attuned to the three-penny opera of tolerance, openness, and pluralism. Not so. We need good labeling so that we don't become careless when handling the dangerous wrapped in inoffensive, inviting packaging. Evil rarely mounts a frontal assault. More likely we are tempted to "the things of Satan" by way of the subliminal. Evil does its work like the song we mindlessly hum after riding the elevator or sitting in the office. The soul is lost in the daily market of compromise.

The angel of Thyatira reminds us that there comes a time when we must stand for something so as not to fall for everything. The cost of discipleship may be the loss of a sale or the end of a friendship. There is a sword which Jesus brings that divides, and requires we choose whom we serve. Costly grace.

The way of Jezebel is separation: inner self hidden from the outer image. This allows for maximum deception. There is a real self, inner and private, which refuses kinship with the onstage persona that faces the world. Nothing sticks. The mask is teflon. Who is this stranger?

The prophets and angels of the Lord counsel a convergence of inner and outer, public and private. There is an integrity that integrates words with deeds, the face in the mirror with that self that only God knows completely. Image and interior embrace. Within, we experience deep calling unto deep.

The fatal attraction to Jezebel is replaced by the faithful commitment of God. And this Divine "yes" for us is spoken as love following upon love, a love which embraces our whole being.

5

Ruth and Naomi:
Friendship

Words can flow easily. Breath rushing up and passing over vocal cords gives us voice. Yet there is a burst of breath, deep and sacred, like Yahweh in the beginning, which reveals who we are. Consider the words of Naomi: "Go back each of you to your mother's house. May the Lord deal kindly with you, as you have dealt with the dead and with me."

These words from the heart are offered to Ruth and Orpah, the daughters-in-law of Naomi. All three women are now sisters in their widowhood. The loss is as painful as it is complete. Naomi, in supreme love, sets them free to begin life anew. Up in age and down on resources, she refuses to play the victim. There has already been too much loss, too much death, and too little hope. For Ruth and Orpah, the best can yet be. Naomi's winged chariot of time rushes onward toward its appointed end, yet she is comforted in knowing that those she loves are protected.

Orpah, amid tears and kisses, departs for her native land of Judah. If Naomi shows us that love which lets go for a higher love, Ruth reveals that love which hangs on for a greater good. However, Naomi does not want the sentiment of the moment to cloud the harsh reality that awaits Ruth, the Moabite: "return after your sister-in-law." Foreigners do not fare well.

But Ruth will never be a foreigner in Israel as long as she is with Naomi. Ruth will never be at home in Moab if Naomi is not by her side. Their friendship transcends geography, religion, and social convention. Their love radiates a warmth that melts the cold barriers that divide. Naomi's words of love are matched by Ruth's words of fidelity: "Do not press me to leave you or to turn back from following you! Where you go, I will go; where you lodge, I will lodge; your people shall be my people; and your God my God. Where you die, I will die—there will I be buried. May the

Lord do thus and so to me, and more as well, if even death parts me from you!"

Words of love which speak of letting go are met by words of fidelity which speak of holding on. These powerful words reveal the fundamental things applied—friendship, commitment, and hope. Yet words have their limits. We know more than we say. We feel deeper than even the poet can express. Words pass into silence: "When Naomi saw that she was determined to go with her, she said no more to her." There is no more to say. Silence speaks its volumes. Action takes over: "So the two of them went on until they came to Bethlehem." It is barley harvest time.

Bible stories are not fairy tales. Scripture characters are not caricatures. The heroic does not cancel the human, all too human. The homecoming is an ironic contrast of rejoicing and resentment. "The whole town of Bethlehem" rushed with joy to welcome home one of its own. Excitement is added with the presence of Ruth. Yet Naomi will have none of it. Emotions have been stuffed down long enough. The dam breaks and her complaint bursts forth: "Call me no longer Naomi, call me Mara, for the Almighty has dealt bitterly with me." Naomi remembers the time of plenty. Now she is empty. The Lord gives and takes away. Bitterness blinds the eye. A cataract forms which does not allow one to see beyond the calamity. Yet a new harvest is about to be gathered. New seeds will be sown, buried away to burst forth. Ruth waits in silence to yield that harvest of life which will turn the bitter, sweet; Mara will become Naomi . . . again.

Naomi is too strong for prolonged self-pity. Out of herself she turns to the needs of Ruth. And Ruth needs a husband. Who better than Naomi's kinsman Boaz? The joyful harvest of the barley season bespeaks a deeper harvest of human love and life. The covenant friendship of Ruth to Naomi is about to connect with the marriage covenant of Ruth and Boaz. Words of fidelity reach climax: "all you say I shall do."

Throughout the journey of Naomi and Ruth we are treated to the story of kindness and fidelity gaining critical mass: kindness begets kindness; fidelity breeds fidelity. Naomi to Ruth to Boaz, so our story goes. And now the God who labors in the shadows of emptiness is about to bring forth a time of bounty.

Boaz, kind and honorable, buys back the lost inheritance of Naomi and wins Ruth as well. Blessed twice over, Boaz and Ruth conceive a child, Obed. And what a child! For Obed perfects the oddity of friendship between Naomi and Ruth. Obed comes through the womb of Ruth and is nursed with the bosom of Naomi. The death of Moab is now healed with this birth at Bethlehem. A blessed hint of *that* birth, declared by the light of a heavenly star and angelic chorus.

Bethlehem to Bethlehem, the continuity of love, human and divine.

For our Obed will be the father of Jesse, the father of David. And the long winding road leads to Jesus. Genealogies are stories with human names and faces giving form and flesh to deep down things: life is connected to life. God works through our human random acts of kindness. From small beginnings, letting go and holding on, God's saving purpose is fulfilled. Ruth, the foreigner, plays her part in the ever inclusive covenant of grace, which perfects law and prophets.

The Apostle teaches that knowledge is incomplete and we see in a mirror dimly. The bonds of friendship we form unfold in ways not imagined. For the mystery that unites separate selves into a whole is with God and grace. Daily commitments, and acts of self-denial, are carried beyond the moment to flourish on distant shores, in far away hearts. Kindness and fidelity ripple out upon a world grown too calm and comfortable with the open-ended. Lives of loyalty shine that light of courageous truth into the dark corners of narrow hearts and closed minds.

In the Fourth Gospel, the soaring story on eagle's wings of Love made visible, Jesus calls those at his Last Supper "friends." With these at table he shared life; now a meal; and with the gift of the Paraclete, a ministry to love as he loved. The legacy of friendship bequeathed to us is no mere sentiment. We dare to say to Jesus and one another: "Where you go, I will go; where you lodge, I will lodge. . . . Where you die, I will die—there will I be buried." And Jesus completes the mystery: "and like the grain of wheat that dies in the earth, I will call you forth to bear much fruit. For where I am there *you* shall be. In dying to self, you shall rise to newness of life."

6

Delilah:
I've Got a Secret

If we always hurt the ones we love, it is because we know where the ones we love hurt. Love means vulnerability. Love runs the risk of overexposure to the warming rays of another's trusting word, touch, or glance. We allow the curtain of our holy of holies to be parted. We are seen as we are. Love is dangerous because we place in the hands of another that fragile, precious mystery called the soul. The slightest hint of rejection, ridicule, or reproach sends us scurrying back into the armor of our well-fortified defenses. We shield ourselves with the promise to never fall in love again. We keep repeating the mantra: "Beware, my foolish heart." The fine line between love and fascination is not easy to discern when blinded by the flash point of desire meeting desire. The wise never rush in and risk the hurt. But neither do the cautious know the exaltation of abandoning oneself into another.

Samson, strong but undisciplined, is a thorn in the side of the powerful Philistines. Who will rid them of this irritant?

Force has failed. A new tactic must be tried. The source of his strength must be uncovered, the secret of his power revealed. However, such knowledge will not come by way of torture but by way of trickery. Again, who?

Onto the stage comes Delilah, whose name means "flirtatious one." The lords of the Philistines use Delilah for their purposes. At least there is light at the end of the tunnel. After all, Samson has a history of wandering eyes and loose lips. He frequents harlots and divulged the answer to his riddle to the women of Timorah. His past paves the way for his future fall.

The process of divulging the secret begins playfully. Samson, initially suspicious of this vixen, joins in the game. He proves to be as deceptive as Delilah. Yet she is not only the mistress of deception, but she also proves to be the model of manipulation. Delilah is determined. The prize is within her grasp. The divulging of the secret is but a deluge of tears away. Delilah strikes at the heart of Samson, hoping to unlock its secret: "How can you say, 'I love you,' when your heart is not with me?" Day after day, Delilah's words work on that heart which protects its secret. The logic of love cannot be long resisted: no secrets between lovers;

lovers share everything;

lovers trust enough to bare all.

The rush of the lion and the charge of the Philistines were nothing compared to the assault of Delilah. The daily water torture of her words and tears washes away Samson's resolve: "And he told her all his mind. . . ."

What strong men could not do, Delilah has accomplished. The secret is out and the strength is gone. Samson's hair is cut. So is his relationship with God. His real strength was through the Spirit, not the power of muscle. The Lord departs and Samson is on his own.

Weak.

Vulnerable.

He has played in Delilah's game and lost. She has found his weakness: undisciplined strength. Samson defeated his external enemies, but could not conquer the enemy within. Delilah was able to get inside his heart and play a deadly game with his head. In her victory, Delilah taunts her trophy: "break free . . . break free." Samson cannot, for the ties that bind are stronger than the bronze fetters. And the strength required for liberation is no longer his.

Samson is now blind and bound; unable to see and no longer free. But the God who departs also returns. The undisciplined strength of Samson is now being schooled through suffering. It is only in his blindness that he comes to see the real source of his strength. As humility and contrition grow in his heart, "the hair on his head begins to grow" as well. The man-child of wanton passion and power becomes the true servant at prayer: "O Lord God, remember me, I pray thee, and strengthen me. . . . I pray . . . that I may be avenged." Samson has been ennobled through his humiliation and suffering. Not only does his strength return, he is now *wise*.

The God of Israel is the God of memory. Sin is always some form of forgetting; redemption involves remembering. Delilah used her guile to sap Samson's strength and render him blind. The Lord remembers the first rush of the Spirit and renews Samson's strength. Delilah's thrill of victory will become the Philistines' agony of defeat. Samson is at once tragic and heroic. In one mighty moment Samson brings down the house and kills the Philistines. Yet there is a price for power. Samson vanquishes his enemies and is vanquished in the process; Samson the tragic. Samson dies as he lived—bringing down his enemies. In this he is heroic. The end was not a contradiction but a summation.

And what of Delilah? Was she consumed by her victory? Justice realized. Did she use her cunning to escape? Not surprised. On this the Bible is silent—a silence which speaks volumes. Maybe the Jews are embarrassed at the spectacle of Samson being bested by a Philistine woman. However, there is a reason which runs deeper. Enduring influences in history do not belong to those who deceive or seduce. Deception undermines trust. Seduction breeds suspicion. Neither builds a lasting foundation or achieves a true victory. The victors are those who, often mistaken as weak and abandoned, are strong in the Lord's Spirit.

As the house comes down on Samson, and Delilah disappears from view, the final episode belongs to the family. Samson's kin come and take his body for burial in the tomb of his father, Manoah. Even in the aftermath of death and destruction, rituals of respect endure: love amid the ruins.

The love of power, through strength or seduction, ultimately blinds and brings down. The power of love alone endures. Such a love, quiet and ordinary, moves through the rubble to bring hope. The invincible spring of the human spirit continues to rise.

Immanuel.

7

Judith:
An Uncommon Valor

If the race does not always go to the swift, neither is the battle always won by the strong—at least not with the strength of rippling muscles or superior numbers. Real strength comes from the Lord who helps the helpless, protects the powerless, and opens the way for the oppressed.

Enter Judith.

A woman of uncommon valor, no ordinary heroine is she. With Judith the mold is broken, and all of our images of the heroic are called into question.

She is a woman, a widow, and expected to be weak. She is supposed to count on the kindness of strangers and pray for the good fortune of finding a protector.

Not Judith.

She is beautiful, intelligent, and counted among the morally upright. All of these will be required if Israel is to be spared and Judith is to play her part in this latest episode of liberation.

The details of the drama are straightforward: Nebuchadnezzar is king and does not take kindly to rivals. In fact, the king believes he is godlike and feels threatened by Yahweh. The king's trusted general, Holofernes, has the Israelites where he wants them—surrounded, and the water is cut off! There is little for Israel to do but cry "ouch" and capitulate.

Judith is waiting in the wings.

The desperate situation of Israel has entered dire straits. Not only is the water running low, but the resolve of the people is nearing empty. Uzziah, the Israelite king, ever the politician, proposes a compromise: hold out for five more days to see if the Lord provides relief. If there is no answer from Yahweh then the town will be turned over to Holofernes. Uzziah is putting pressure on Yahweh to find a way out of this tight spot. After all, what will the nations say if Yahweh lets his people knuckle under to the local bully?

Enter Yahweh through Judith.

Yes, Yahweh will respond, but not according to the expectations of Uzziah. In the face of impending disaster, the Lord reveals himself to be the supreme ironist. This national hero is not found on the barricades or among those dressed for battle. Yahweh turns to two women—Judith and her maid.

The portrait of Judith is painted with deep irony: a woman of wealth, she lives simply; a woman of beauty, she lives as a celibate; a woman of virtue, she plays on the moral weakness of men; a childless widow, her courage gives rebirth to the people. And Judith is a woman of her time who dares to take charge of a desperate situation.

God, the Supreme Ironist.

Judith's first challenge is to convince Uzziah that his compromise is really a capitulation. In a stirring speech she preaches truth to the timid and courage to the cowardly. Judith refuses to be frozen by fear. What is required is action. Faith in Yahweh must be matched with human initiative. To let the Lord do it all is the sin of presumption. This passivity, parading as virtue, is really to put the Lord to the test. But as Judith teaches Uzziah, it is the Lord "who is putting us to the test, just as he did to our ancestors."

Judith must now turn from the timidity of Uzziah to the moral threat posed by Holofernes. Choice of weapons? The tongue is mightier than the sword. Words inflict invisible wounds that no balm can heal. The action of Judith will be done through the words she speaks. "Please, please, God . . . Grant me a beguiling tongue for wounding and bruising those who have terrible designs against your covenant and your sacred house."

Judith arrives.

So far Judith's actions have been in words: preaching to Uzziah and praying to Yahweh. Now her words turn to action. Judith prepares for the battle: off comes sackcloth and the widow's dress, replaced with a tiara and clothes which excite the male imagination and turn women's heads with envy, as they hold tight to their husbands. Her beautiful body, revealing and hiding just enough, is made more desirable with the aroma from a fresh bath and rich perfume. This human work of art is completed with the adornments of sandals, bracelets, rings, earrings: the jewelry required for victory.

The power of woman is the power to disarm. If beauty does not kill the beast, it certainly soothes the savage breast. Judith is stunning. Her inner and outer beauty are one. She leaves the men of Bethulia behind their city walls. Judith makes her way to Holofernes when an Assyrian patrol takes her into custody. Judith tells these men she must see Holofernes so he can "conquer all the hill country without risking life or limb of his men." There is no defense against Judith's beauty. Mesmerized, the Assyrians provide Judith and her maid with an escort for protection. Beauty is dangerous.

Judith stoops to conquer.

The lustful Holofernes receives the pious Judith. The dance of this dangerous liaison commences. Is Judith overmatched? The tension is unbearable. Judith proves to be a master at playing the prideful Holofernes. He becomes completely disarmed in the presence of feminine beauty, intelligence, courage, and strength. Against these there is no defense. It is Judith who takes the lead and calls the tune. Masterfully, she gains power by pretending to be powerless. She flatters by seeming to be flattered. She is admired by claiming to admire the greatness of Holofernes. The general invites the widow into his tent. The end is near.

Holofernes is intoxicated by a mixture of beauty and wine. The prospect of a double conquest—the Jews and Judith—sends his head reeling. With two spirit-filled blows by Judith, this becomes literally true!

Exit Judith.

She and the maid leave the Assyrian camp with their trophy. Once among her people, Judith gives public display to her prize, which produces courage in the soldiers. The power of woman is not only to disarm but to empower. The once timid men of Israel follow the example of Judith and charge into action. The Assyrians are defeated. Israel, as in the time of Exodus, is liberated.

Judith is enshrined.

The heroism of Judith is theological and epic. Yahweh chooses the weak and makes them strong for his work of liberation. Judith's conquest was a triumph for Israel. Her personal wish was for national security. Her beauty was in the service of virtue. All the spoils of victory Judith offers to the Lord in a song of praise: "I will sing to my God a new song: Lord, you are great and glorious, Marvelous in strength, invincible." In being self-forgetful, Judith is remembered for the ages.

One of Judith's last acts before she dies is to free her maid.

The power of woman is to disarm.

The power of woman is to empower.

The power of woman is to liberate.

8

Bathsheba:
An Affair to Remember

Solomon's star is on the rise. He has ascended to the throne of his father, David. The real king-maker, however, is Solomon's mother. The hand that rocked the cradle has placed her son at the center of Israel's power elite. Though in the twilight of her years, Solomon's mother continues to wield influence and sits at his right hand. And who is this mother of Solomon? This maker of kings? This confidant who retains influence to the end?

Bathsheba!

Time is a mystery, its unfolding, a grace. The early years don't always reveal what is to be. It is only in the evening of our days, the season of harvest, that seeds planted early flower. So it is with Bathsheba.

We first see the young Bathsheba through the roving eye of the restless king David. He is not at the battleline against the Ammonites but at the homefront. Yet there is a contest to commence: David with himself. Unable to rest, David roams the palace rooftop. His eyes spot a beautiful woman bathing. He sends a messenger to inquire. She is Bathsheba, the wife of Uriah, a trusted warrior in David's army. Another expedition by David's agents results in Bathsheba being brought to the king. Exercising the royal prerogative of the day, David sleeps with Bathsheba. It is her turn to send a message to David: "I'm pregnant."

What is to be done? What the powerful often do—coverup. Uriah is recalled from the front under the guise of David's concern for the troops. Vice seeks the cover of virtue. The real reason emerges: Uriah will sleep with Bathsheba. The lust of David will be buried in the normal urge of Uriah for his wife. How clever. Yet the best laid plans . . .

Uriah's piety foils the plans of David. Soldiers refrained from sexual intercourse during times of battle. The ritual purity of Uriah prevents the coverup of David and Bathsheba's sexual impurity. One more try. David gets Uriah drunk. Of course strong drink will weaken resolve and Uriah will take Bathsheba. One more failure. Uriah sleeps with the servants. He never makes it home.

David becomes desperate. If the deed cannot be buried, then Uriah will be. David draws Joab, Uriah's superior, into the swirling eddy of moral decay. The coverup will be completed through a setup. Uriah will be sent into the fieriest of the fighting. At the opportune time, support will be withdrawn. The valiant but vulnerable Uriah will be slain. At last the mission is accomplished. Uriah is slain. No one will know.

Interlude.

David is in the clear. The business of ruling and warring are to continue as usual. Not so. Even the king is subject to the higher moral law of God. The scales of justice are imbalanced and the Lord's anointed must render an account before the One who reads thoughts and knows hearts. Nathan, God's prophet, is sent to speak truth to power. Through the prophet's parable, the wickedness of David is uncovered: he is the man! The Bible is blunt. There is no attempt to put a positive spin on David's sin, no explanation, no rationalization. David slept with Bathsheba and had Uriah killed.

Prelude to Bathsheba.

Sin cannot be cloistered. Wickedness is not private. Lust leads to murder. The logic of evil works its way to deadly consequences. The powerless and innocent too often suffer the after-shocks of the mighty's arrogance. Confession and contrition are necessary but not sufficient. The legacy of sin endures; its effects linger.

Bathsheba emerges.

Bathsheba exists in the shadows of strong men. She is the wife of Uriah. She is taken by David as property by royal prerogative. After a decent interval of mourning, David *brings* Bathsheba to *his* house so she can be *his* wife and give birth to *his* son. With David she is more passive than permissive. Yet the Bible makes no effort to excuse. Passivity carries responsibility. Hence, Bathsheba must share in the consequences of *their* sin.

The child of David and Bathsheba is taken from them by Yahweh. The wages of sin is death. The innocent suffer. Few experiences are as peak as the birth of a child. Few losses are as agonizing as the death of one's flesh. Such a tragedy either draws the couple closer or drives spouses apart; either way, their relationship is never the same. The individuals are forever changed.

David comforts Bathsheba. Their suffering brings them together. Their marital love brings forth a son whom "Yahweh loved." He receives two names: one private, Jedidiah ("Beloved One of Yahweh"). The other name of this child is public or the throne name, Solomon (from the Hebrew *selo-moh*, "his replacement"). The Lord who took away now gives. This child is to be the beloved who will replace the one lost to sin. True repentance gives birth to new life.

Epilogue.

Bathsheba does not appear again until near the end of David's reign. The lost years of Bathsheba between Solomon's birth and his enthronement are not wasted years. The hiddenness of this time does not preclude a revelation about Bathsheba. For when we encounter her again, she is planning with Nathan to place Solomon on the throne. Once on the throne, Bathsheba exercises her great influence on behalf of others before her son-king. The passive Bathsheba of long ago is no more. She is now mature in years, having been aged in the crucible of suffering and loss. Yet Bathsheba has emerged a woman of strength. No mere survivor, Bathsheba is a woman of nobility.

History is written by winners, who are rarely women. The Gospel of Matthew opens with the genealogy of Jesus. The story of his ancestors includes the following: "And David was the father of Solomon by the wife of Uriah" (Mt 1:6). *By the wife of Uriah*. Bathsheba is nameless and preserved in terms of her role in relation to her husband. The last to be buried is the past. It is part of the permanent record: even though Uriah had died and David took Bathsheba as his lawful wife, the sin remains. Revisionist history has been kind to King David; not so to "the wife of Uriah." Yet what cannot be revised is the presence of Bathsheba within the history of Israel and the story of Jesus. God's union with humanity includes the fidelity of Ruth and the infidelity of Bathsheba. Both are found within our heart and history. God works with each for a greater grace.

So it was. So it is. So it will be.

9

Esther:
A Shared Courage

If to be great is to be misunderstood, then Esther is indeed great, for she is highly misunderstood—and often unappreciated. To put it mildly, Esther has played to mixed reviews. The Essene community at Qumran did not regard the book of Esther as canonical. The only book of the Hebrew Scriptures absent from the Dead Sea scrolls is Esther. However, Maimonides (1135-1204 A.D.), the great Jewish scholar, ranks only the Pentateuch ahead of Esther in importance.

When it comes to the Christian reception of Esther, the embrace is no less mixed. In the East, Christians often did not accept Esther as canonical. By contrast, the West usually afforded Esther canonical status. Yet Martin Luther lumped Esther with II Maccabees and proclaimed: "I am so hostile to this book [II Maccabees] and to Esther that I wish they did not exist at all; for they judaize too greatly and have much pagan impropriety."

Among those who disdain Esther there is a common complaint, namely, the absence of any mention of God's name. In fact, the king of Persia is alluded to 190 times; Yahweh receives neigh a nod. Compounding the complaint is the absence of essential Judaism: Covenant, Law, Temple, sacrifice, and virtue. The only overtly religious component is the relatively unimportant discipline of fasting.

The question: Is there a message, easily missed, from Esther? Yes. And the key to unlocking Esther's wisdom comes by joining her to Judith. These sisters-in-heroism are joined at the heart by their devotion to God and their dedication to the Jewish nation.

In a previous portrait, the beauty and courage of Judith were unveiled. Her heroism was celebrated without a discouraging word. The explanation is found in her explicit devotion to Yahweh. Before, during, and after her work of liberating Israel, Judith constantly turns to the Lord for strength.

She rejoices in her role as the Lord's instrument of deliverance. There is no doubt that Yahweh is *acting through* Judith.

Not so with Esther. A brief summary of her story follows.

A beauty contest is held in order to replace the reluctant Queen Vashti, who refuses to play King Xeres' chauvinistic game. The queen would rather be banished than perform in order to please her pompous consort. The king starts a search for a worthy replacement. The winner: Esther, who is popular, beautiful, smart, and oh yes, Jewish. No fool this Esther, she hides her Jewishness from Xeres. Brains and beauty meet in this Esther; she reveals a plot to kill Xeres. No ingrate this king, he promises to grant just about any request.

Enter the villain of our story, Haman. He hates Jews and persuades Xeres to sign an edict that would exterminate them all. While at a dinner given by Esther for Xeres and her enemy Haman, Esther makes known her request and reveals the corruption of Haman. She pleads with Xeres not to exterminate the Jews. This is her request. Esther reveals that Haman has abused his friendship with Xeres and even violates social rules by daring to touch her. This is her revelation. Haman is executed on the gallows he constructed to exterminate the Jews. The king cannot rescind his edict to exterminate the Jews, but he allows the Jews to defend themselves and government officials to aid in their defense. The Jews emerge victorious and celebrate the feast of Purim—a time of deliverance and feasting. In both her request and her revelation, Esther, with the help of friend and foe, saves the Jewish people. The victory comes through human effort. Yahweh is not mentioned.

This shut-out of Yahweh does not sit well with those who demand their religion straight up, undiluted by the iced water rocks of human complexity. Yet the Bible serves no such brew. Many ingredients are required. God is always present but not always seen. Yahweh often speaks loudest when he is silent. The Lord becomes most visible when the only agents appear to be human. All of these combined into producing a masterpiece, a portrait that grabs our attention by attracting us to what (who) is missing. The very hiddenness of God makes our search for him all the more intense. The silence of Yahweh attunes the hearing heart for any word from the Lord. A story so obviously human sharpens our eye for any hint of grace.

The portrait of Judith's heroism is painted on the canvas of explicit religion, with the bright colors of Yahweh's domination. The Lord is in charge. The portrait of Esther's courage is etched on the canvas of an implied faith that hasn't quite found its color, form, or texture. Where is the Lord? Unlike the summer faith of Judith, there is a reserve about Esther which gives rise to that tension between despair and hope. With Esther, snow blankets the earth with a sprinkling of spring birds. Each season of nature, and human heart and history, tells its tale of which triumphs and which recedes into the eternal winter.

The mature unveiling of the courageous heart reveals a complex canvas on which both Judith and Esther appear. The heroism of Judith can be perverted into a presumption, a passive voice, which lets God do it all. The courage of Esther can be diverted into an arrogance, hyperactive voice, which claims, "*I did it all, my way.*" Yet, when joined together, they provide the antidote which gives life.

God's people are always in danger of annihilation. To follow the Lord is to live on the edge and walk in the dark valley. The threatened holocaust of Haman is a permanent feature of history and casts a deep shadow on the twentieth century.

The gallows of Haman and those at Flossenburg attest to the enduring presence of evil, an evil which is only magnified by the "good" men and women who do nothing.

To defeat evil requires the power of God *and* the courage of human beings. We need the heroism of Judith who finds voice for prayer. We know they prayed at Auschwitz. We need the courage of those like Esther who simply *do* what *is* right because it is right. We need that human protest against inhumanity which recognizes a common dignity and a shared destiny, though it may not be able to give voice to its righteous anger. We need that protest of prayer which proclaims with the Psalmist, "My times are in your hand; deliver me from the hand of my enemies and persecutors!" (Ps. 31:15).

Esther is more of a verb than a noun, a predicate rather than a subject. The story is short on character analysis and long on action. We know the *who* of Esther by *what* she does. Her lack of reflection, introspection, and even explicit prayer does not denote an absence of faith. It is simply the demands of a dire situation, impending extermination, which requires reflex action. Reflex can give way to reflection—later! For now there is work to be done. That Yahweh is not mentioned does not mean God is absent, only silent. Not every victory over evil is able to be vocalized to the tune of praise the Lord. Yet it is a triumph nonetheless. It is often for others, survivors and progeny, to see the hand of God and sing the hymns of praise.

Heroism is often hidden in the marrow of the ordinary and buried in the banality of the everyday. The courage to be kind is found in the heroism of giving water to the thirsty, a hand to the lost. It is in clothing the naked, a voice raised for the voiceless. It is burying the dead, a cry of protest, "Never again," "We shall overcome." In these, and countless other episodes, we find ourselves joined with the explicit faith of the born again and the moral passion of the humanly concerned. God unites both for his victory of goodness.

A knowing smile steals across the faces of Judith and Esther.

10

Deborah:
Mother in Israel

In poetry and prose the story of Deborah is preserved for the ages. Deborah is a woman who is revealed through her roles and revered for her leadership ability. Deborah is both judge and prophetess; she is prudent in human affairs and wise in the ways of God. Both roles unite in this extraordinary woman, to provide Israel with a leader who is able to size up the situation and seize the moment. Victory requires both vision and prudence, inspiration and preparation, a sense of the big picture and respect for the practical.

At the time of Deborah, Israel is a loose confederation in the hostile land of Canaan. The Canaanites are superior in numbers and technology (the chariot). Baraq ("Lightning"), Israel's general, is more flash than substance. Frankly, he is timid, hesitant, and lacking in faith. Baraq is more focused on the enemy than he is on his own resources. He becomes paralized by what he lacks rather than being energized by the promise of the Lord. Baraq cannot, will not, attack. Yet the moment is ripe for victory. If only someone will step up and lead the Lord's troops forward.

Do times give birth to leaders? Do leaders shepherd events for their own designs? Where is the Lord of history to be found: in the person? In the challenge? In both? How so?

Such questions must be put on hold in favor of the demands of the moment. Speculation must step aside for action. The window of victory does not remain forever open. History contains the tragedy caused by the timid. Into the breach steps Deborah. Her immediate challenge is to rouse Baraq out of his paralysis. The prophetess points to the Lord's oracle, which promised victory. The Lord will conquer the chariots of the Canaanites' general, Sisera. If only . . .

Admittedly, Baraq's "whim of iron" is no match for the iron chariots of

Sisera. What to do? Deborah talks a good game, but will she walk her talk? There may be a way out of this after all. Baraq turns to Deborah with the following condition: "If you go with me, I'll go. But if you don't go with me, I won't go." There. That ought to silence the woman. This "challenge" will return her to her place: in the shade of her own tree, judging the daily disputes in the people's court.

Surprise! Surprise! "Certainly, I will go with you." Deborah's theological certitude—Yahweh has promised victory—trumps Baraq's condition-ridden response. The battle commences. Once again Baraq hesitates. Once more Deborah comes to the rescue: "Up! This is the day in which Yahweh has put Sisera in your power! Does not Yahweh advance before you?" Baraq descends Mount Tabor to engage Sisera. Better to fight the chariots of Sisera than face the wrath of Deborah!

Through the power of Yahweh, Baraq enjoys victory. Sisera flees. He is taken in by Jael. She promises hospitality and safety. Instead, Jael takes a tent peg and, with a mallet in hand, pounds the peg into Sisera's neck. "He twitched convulsively and died." As Sisera breathes his last, Baraq arrives in familiar fashion—late and out of breath. Once again the indecisive Baraq benefits because of the decisive (though brutal) action of a woman.

There is a theological bottom line which emerges: Yahweh is all powerful and faithful to his promises. Trust, not timidity, wins the day.

The prose of Deborah gives way to poetry; the narrative breaks into song. Once again we know Deborah by her role, "a mother in Israel!" This is not just poetic license. Deborah, judge and prophetess, has become "a mother in Israel." Admittedly, at first blush, the mention of motherhood within the context of a war story seems out of place. Yet on closer inspection, motherhood is intimately connected with the history of war. Countless are the tears which have been shed by mothers over the spilled blood of sons and daughters. No one suffers more because of war than the women whose wombs bore, and breasts nursed, the finest flowers of each nation who gather on the field of battle.

Deborah, whose name means "Honey Bee," is praised as a "mother in Israel." She, like her namesake, provides nurturing, nourishment, and sweetness to her children, the people of Israel. Deborah's tears are those of joy because sons are safe and daughters protected. Yet there is a salt in all tears which bespeaks a flavoring sadness that rounds out the reality of life. The joy and triumph of mother Deborah is balanced by the pathos of Sisera's mother, who waits for the son who will not return. Her story touches the heart of all, especially mothers, who wait for the one who comes not.

Women are good at waiting. At least women acquire a good deal of practice: motherhood; the right suitor; men returning from the fields and from war; illness to heal; birth; and death. The life of women is very much a life of waiting. There is a wisdom bestowed through waiting, a strength of character formed by delaying gratification. The power of women is the ability to endure; long suffering is a loving which ennobles the soul.

Sisera is murdered by Jael. Her glee is starkly contrasted with the agony of Sisera's mother. The battle is long spent. The time for troops to return has passed. Why does he delay? Doesn't Sisera know how anxious his mother is for the cloud of dust raised by his returning chariot? Yet there is no sight or sound of the chariot. The road offers no hope for this mother, who labors mightily to repress the growing realization of death. Death is intellectually accepted but existentially rejected: "Death comes for everyone. Except for *my* loved ones. Except for *me*."

The royal attendants join in the conspiracy of denial. Sisera delays because the spoils of victory are so great. Their wisdom is a foolishness which tries to shield, from loved ones and superiors, painful truths. In the most wrenching of ironies, the neck of Sisera is not adorned by the spoils of victory but is pierced by the peg of Jael.

The Song of Deborah is silent about the reaction of this unnamed mother when the dreadful news of death is finally delivered. Words are meaningless. This mother is Every Mother. Her pathos transcends the barriers of race and religion, gender and geography. Heart touches heart, a heart wounded deeply into the evening of her years.

Deborah's poetry concludes with a prayer. May Yahweh's enemies perish. May the lovers of Yahweh "be like the sunburst in full strength!" May we also harbor a hope for that time when mothers will no longer wait for that son who does not return and that daughter lost to war. May the Song of Deborah mature into the lyrics of Isaiah: "they shall beat their swords into plowshares, and their spears into prunning hooks; nation shall not lift a sword against nation, neither shall they learn war any more" (Is. 2:4).

11

Tamar:
Victim, Victorious

Tamar is not timid. Initially a victim, she emerges gloriously victorious. There was abundant reason for Tamar to accept her fate. All the forces of law, tradition, religion, and social structure are marshaled against her. Yet Tamar proved to be "the mouse that roared." Her story offers hope for all who find themselves trapped in oppressive structures.

Tamar, a Canaanite woman, is selected by Judah to marry his eldest son, Er. Unfortunately, Er "greatly offended" Yahweh and dies. The wages of sin is death. Next in line for the hand of Tamar is Onan, who meets with a similar fate because of his sin ("he wasted his seed on the ground, to avoid contributing offspring for his brother"). There is one brother left for Tamar, and Judah is not about to trust his final son to a similar fate. Never two without three. There is only one thing to do: Judah sends Tamar back to her father's house a childless widow. The long way home is one of disgrace. What started out with so much promise ends in rejection. The names Er ("childless one") and Onan ("grief") clearly capture the plight of Tamar—she is childless but pregnant with grief.

Tamar is the victim. She is a pawn in the system which treats women as property. Judah selected Tamar to be the wife of his eldest son. Her consent is not required; her feelings are not considered. After Er dies, Tamar becomes the responsibility and obligation of Onan. He must marry Tamar in order to continue the blood line. Even after death, the interests of Er (a sinner done in by Yahweh) take precedence over the unknown preference of Tamar. She is further insulted by an ingenious offer from Judah to marry his last son, Shelah, who is too young. The commitment of Judah to Tamar has become a charade. This last-gasp offer by Judah rings hollow. Tamar goes home.

Tamar, widowed and childless, knows the pain of shame. Modern cries

61

of "unfair!" "you poor victim," "you have rights" do not register in this previous age and foreign culture. And even if they did, Tamar is too substantial for such cheerleading. Tamar rejects the role of victim. Such a status only increases her powerlessness. Tamar will wait for events to break her way. Time and tide will join to provide her with the opportunity to triumph.

Tamar's patience pays off. After a decent interval of mourning the loss of his wife, Judah takes a business trip with Shelah, who is now grown. Tamar gets wind of this trip to his sheepshearers. At last she can discard her widow's weeds. She dons the disguise of a harlot. By the roadside she lies in wait for Judah. He does not disappoint. He propositions her in the old-fashioned way: "Come, let me have intercourse with you." The proposition bespeaks a price—a kid to be sent at a future date. Enjoy now; pay later. Not so fast. Tamar knows well how fast and loose Judah is with the truth. The future payment will require a present pledge. More than words, Tamar requests some tangible sign of the transaction. Three, to be specific: seal, cord, and staff. This trinity touches on the identity of Judah as a man of judicial and pastoral power. The staff is a symbol of the promised Messiah who will shepherd the people of God. In time, Tamar will come to play her part in salvation history. For now she must be content to let nature take its course.

Tamar is pregnant. Her condition can no longer be concealed. Word of her "harlotry" reaches Judah, who reacts with typical moral outrage. Her "sin" is understood as an affront against Judah and his family. The old double standard is in overdrive: Tamar is required to refrain from sex since she was *given* to Shelah after his two brothers died. However, she never became his wife in fact. The double standard reveals a single obligation: Tamar is obligated and must face a fiery death. Judah and Shelah are fancy free.

But they are not quite as free as first appears. The past is about to become present. Tamar is prepared to play the trump card—three cards, to be exact: Judah's seal, cord, and staff. Making virtue a necessity, Judah admits both his paternity and the righteousness of Tamar. He failed to fulfill the custom concerning the marriage of Shelah to Tamar. The twins of Tamar, Perez and Zerah, are Judah's as well.

Subsequent history unfolds in favor of Judah, and Tamar by extension, for it is Judah who receives the coveted blessing of Jacob (Gen 49). It is Perez, the son of Judah *and* Tamar, who is the ancestor of David (Ruth 4:18-22; 1 Chronicles 2:5-15). Tamar the Canaanite and Ruth the Moabite are foreigners joined in the story of salvation. Each in her own way is an ancestor of the great king David. In the fullness of time it will be revealed that both these women are the ancestors of the King of Kings (Mt 1:3,5).

The story of Tamar teaches that liberation is not always achieved at the barricades or through taking to the streets. There can be a quiet, inner revolution which has its genesis in the imagination. The power of the idea whose time has come achieves a conquest for minds and hearts which no army can conquer.

Tamar is a person of her time, caught in all its trappings. Yet she conceives of herself as more than a victim, a mere object of an unjust situation. The cards dealt from the cultural deck can be reshuffled. We don't always have to play the hand assigned. Tamar's rebellion in the intellect shatters the stereotypes of women as desire-driven and mind-deficient. Her eventual victory over victimhood is a tribute to Tamar's ability to plan, calculate, and work within a structure to her advantage. A prudent playing of the system is a game not limited to men only. Tamar knew what to ask for from Judah as a pledge. She knew how to play the pledge when the time came.

Not only does Tamar's story teach that liberation is mental, but also that the righting of wrongs takes time. Swift justice may only increase the damage and the body count. Years pass before her plan of vindication yields victory. There is a strength of character and discipline of temperament which bides time. Tamar waited years for Judah to take his trip. Her patience paid off.

Tamar is a figure at once familiar and strange. We easily identify with the woman wronged by men and unjust social structures. We see in her struggle the cry of the oppressed and the victimization of the weak. Tamar appears on the evening news and plays a prominent role in our daily newspapers.

Tamar is strange to our age. She rebels at once against her status as childless widow, as well as against the unfair situation of the double standard. However, her rebellion is one of patient planning and the prudence to seize the moment. Tamar looks for neither instant justice nor a victim status which excuses as it keeps one perpetually powerless. Tamar's strength is her ability to wait. Her wisdom is knowing the opportune time to act. There is a retreat which prepares the victim for victory.

Tamar's gift to us comes more from what is strange than what is familiar.

12

Susanna:
Guilty Until Proven Innocent

The power of a good story is its ability to draw us into its world of relationships, meaning, and outcome. We do more than understand the story line and the characters; we *care*. As the pages turn we are drawn into the magic of that willing suspension of disbelief. Few narratives grip the imagination and "turn the page" with the intensity of a mystery story. It's the Perry Mason in all of us. We *must* find out "who done it."

The mystery story challenges our ability to uncover the truth which is present but hidden. Clues are collected so that the obvious is revealed as obviously wrong. The prime suspect turns out to be innocent. The least suspected is exposed as the guilty party. In the end virtue triumphs over vice; truth and justice prevail; the innocent are set free; and the guilty are served their just desserts. God is in his heaven and all is right with the world . . . at least in the cosmos of the mystery writer.

The Bible contains a gem of a mystery story. It involves the beautiful and virtuous Susanna, caught in the lustful lies of men in high places protected by their powerful positions. Questions abound: will the power of position prove mightier than the power of truth? Will virtue overcome villainy? How will the wrong fail and the right prevail? How will the Lord write straight with the crooked lines of perverted passion? These keep us involved.

The everyday world of Susanna is one of privilege and predictability. Her upbringing was grounded in being upright in the sight of the Lord. Marriage continued this life of virtue. Susanna's husband, Joakim, is numbered among the rich and influential. There is a *quid pro quo* between moral goodness and material goods. Susanna has been twice blessed: good parents in a loving home and a good husband who maintains the style to which she has become accustomed. Susanna's world contains no surprises.

Until now. On one ordinary summer's day, Susanna enjoys an ordinary pleasure—a bath. Yet lurking in the garden were two lustful old men whose passion grew as hot as the noonday's sun. They had been training for their treachery for some time. They were known to Susanna and her husband. These men were elders and judges! They used Joakim's home as a courthouse to dispense justice. Over time their thoughts turned from God. They allowed instinct to rule intellect, passion to suppress conscience, and the leering eye to darken the soul. Day after day they took their positions of passion to look at Susanna. They looked with violence upon Susanna, an object of pleasure, watched for the opportune time.

Susanna's world is about to be shaken to the foundations. She is about to see that wealth does not save; passion can pervert position; reputation is fragile; virtue does not spare one from suffering; legality can be misused to cover up immorality; and friends can be the most deadly of enemies.

Out of the cover of the garden rush the two elders to expose their intentions: "Look, the garden door is shut, and no one can see us. We are burning with desire for you; so give your consent, and lie with us. If you refuse, we will testify against you that a young man was with you, and this was why you sent your maids away." Their passion is to the point: consent or be condemned.

What's a girl to do?

Their straightforward proposition is countered by Susanna's uncompromising response: "I choose not to do it; I will fall into your hands, rather than sin in the sight of the Lord." Yet, just saying "no" has dire consequences—death. The law can be perverted to do the bidding of passion.

The elders go public with their tale of Susanna's "adultery." The home of her happiness now becomes the courthouse of her condemnation. In the presence of those who once extolled her virtue and beauty, Susanna now hears the declaration of her guilt. Though innocent, Susanna is about to be stoned. The lustful lies of the elders wins the verdict simply because they *are* elders and judges. Position determines perception, which yields the judgment of death. The logic of lust reaches its mortal conclusion: Susanna must be killed.

There is one final appeal to the court, justice, and Judge from whom no heart is closed or thought hidden. Susanna's world lies in shambles but her faith remains strong. Throughout this charade of a court, Susanna has been silent. Now at the end she finds her voice. It is not the cry for a new trial, but the protest of prayer to the only One whose verdict matters: "O eternal God, you know what is secret and aware of all things before they came to be; you know that these men have given false evidence against me. And now I am to die, though I have done none of the wicked things that they have charged against me."

What's a God to do?

Susanna's eleventh-hour appeal does not go unanswered. God acts in terms of justice, not clemency. Into the midst of these corrupt proceedings, the Lord convenes his own court. Through the Holy Spirit, Daniel condemns the condemners. Under intense cross-examination, the wickedness of the elders is exposed. The tangled web of deception has trapped its spinners. The innocent Susanna is set free. The fate which awaited our heroine is now assigned to our villains. The assembly which was quick to condemn Susanna turns on a dime and raises "a great shout and blessed God, who saves those who hope in him."

In effect, group-think rarely yields truth. Everyone loves a winner. The assembly blessed God. The parents of Susanna, along with her husband, praised the Lord for such a moral person. And Daniel enjoyed in the esteem of the people.

All's well that ends well.

Yet we know that while Susanna's saga ends, the themes linger on in history. Women, against their will, are still forced to "consent" to men of power and position. The vulnerable find themselves trapped in sinful social structures. The custodians of the public trust too often champion private interests over the common good. The mighty misuse their status to exploit the weak and sway public opinion away from justice.

The prayer of Susanna for vindication continues throughout history. The cries of the oppressed make their way to the ears of the Lord. God raises up Daniel in each age to confront the mighty on their thrones and the powerful in their conceit. It must never be forgotten why we remember Susanna: she is a woman of prayer. And without prayer there is no divine intervention, vindication, and restoration of honor.

Susanna is a reminder to an age which likes to take to the streets and rush to the barricades, shouting that prayer is powerful. The Lord of creation and history loves justice above sacrifices. Through prayer the Holy Spirit raises up men and women who hunger and thirst after righteousness.

Such as Susanna.

Such as Daniel.

Such is the Kingdom of God.

13

Elizabeth:
My Reproach

Elizabeth is barren but blameless. Though absent of child, Zechariah and Elizabeth are counted among the "upright in God's sight" and blameless before those who know them best. Yet the reproach remains: no child, no *male* child. And the biological clock has struck the twelfth hour. Fertility is a futile hope.

Elizabeth is the first woman mentioned in the New Testament. She will continue a tradition present in the Old Testament: a childless woman who gives birth to a son through the grace of God. Sarah to Hannah to Elizabeth, so goes the story of the God through whom nothing is impossible. Isaac to Samson to John, each playing a key part in salvation history.

But this is jumping ahead. The evangelist Luke raises the curtain on our couple with Zechariah attending to his priestly duties. As the incense rises to the Lord, the angel Gabriel announces that Zechariah's prayer has risen and been heard. God has responded; Elizabeth's reproach will be removed. The barren will once again burst forth with new life. The Lord's time of grace has healed Elizabeth's period of disgrace.

Heavenly speech yields human silence. Gabriel's message is met by Zechariah's doubt. Only at the time of fulfillment will Zechariah find his voice. The innermost thoughts of Elizabeth become one with the innermost miracle of life developing in her womb. The vision given to Zechariah in the temple has taken flesh in the body-temple of Elizabeth. The Lord liberates: "he saw fit to take away the disgrace I have endured among people."

Life shows itself. Its good news is meant for telling. Mary goes in happy haste to be with her kinswoman Elizabeth. There is a bond beyond blood; it is the cord of grace which binds in spirit and truth. Annunciation to annunciation; life to life; herald to herald. In their common story, Mary and Elizabeth find their voices as sisters-in-praise. Canticle meets canticle; the great things God has done burst forth in song. With a joyful jump, the life within Elizabeth heralds the One who is life itself.

Here we are privileged to witness a revelation at once human and divine. The gathering of mothers; the sharing of joy. The bonding of women in their power to give birth; the revelation of grace upon grace. Different lives: a common story in God's salvation history.

After the singing comes the daily living. The excitement of their shared favor gives way to the reality of *being* pregnant. For the young Mary this means morning sickness, weight gain, and the ever-present danger of miscarriage. For the up-in-years Elizabeth this means a radical change of routine in the twilight of her life. Together they will supply what is lacking in the other. These mothers will be one in their pregnancy as their sons will be one, each in his own way, in their work for the Kingdom of God. At the same time their coming together includes a departure; intense intimacy knows separation. In time their sons' paths will cross; short but intense. And at the end each goes his prescribed way to the glory of God.

Elizabeth, long cursed, is now twice blessed: she delivers a son. God's promise has been realized. The community celebrates her joy. The celebration culminates with the circumcision, naming, and revelation of John's future ministry. For when the newborn is named, Zechariah's mouth is opened and he praises God. All present are filled with awe. The events of the day become the talk of the town and the topic of conversation: "Now what is this child to become?"

The destiny of this child cannot be separated from the woman who gave him life. Elizabeth is mentioned no more, and the story of John is yet to unfold. Yet her presence is as strong as it is silent. In all that this last herald and prophet of Yahweh will accomplish, the influence of Elizabeth is revealed. There is a sacred bond, strong and deep, between mother and son. Time, distance, and death will not break this cord that ties.

Even Luke, the most woman-friendly of the Gospel, identifies John as he begins his public ministry as "the son of Zechariah." The influence of history and culture are not easily transcended. However, the nurturing of a mother finds it way into the marrow of a son. As the ministry of John unfolds, we see Elizabeth in John—and never more so than at the hour of death!

The public ministry of John is often portrayed as one of sound and moral fury. John confronts the power elite with the message of conversion. At first he is met with curiosity and amusement. Ridicule can be effective in silencing those who make us uncomfortable. In addition, the strange dress and diet of this "voice crying in the wilderness" only add to the oddness. However, in time, curiosity and amusement wear thin. Ridicule only serves to encourage this incorrigible one. He must be made to pay the ultimate price. And so he will. And does.

Yet the measure of John, and the abiding influence of Elizabeth, are revealed in three episodes on the way to martyrdom. John knows who he is and what he is about. The attention given to him and his message does not go to his ego. John is not the messiah. He is the voice of preparation; the preliminary herald to the primary Proclaimer.

The second window into John's soul is raised at the river Jordan. The one who baptizes with water proclaims the One who baptizes with fire. There is no "turf war." Out of the crowd comes the One who is clean all over; yet here he stands before John. Eyes meet. Hearts beat. Heaven speaks: "This is my beloved Son, with whom I am well pleased."

John the herald—John the baptizer—evokes echoes of voices past. Who does not recognize the voice of Elizabeth being resurrected on the banks of this river? For she was visited by Mary, the Mother of her Lord, and now *that* Lord visits her son. Elizabeth's recognition of Mary's superior privilege is replayed in John's recognition of Jesus as the one "whose sandals he is not fit to untie." John must decrease so Jesus can increase. This selfless surrender to the next phase of salvation was learned in the womb. Elizabeth, in the power of the Spirit, proclaims Mary blest along with the fruit of her womb. John, in the power of the Spirit, proclaims Jesus "the lamb of God" (Jn 1:36). Lesson taught. Lesson learned.

Elizabeth knew from the first that her son was meant for some special work of God. Built in to the removal of her reproach was the understanding that John belonged to salvation history. Each passing day he grew strong in spirit, anticipating the day he would leave for his mission. Each day Elizabeth surrended the joy of her old age; she schooled John in his need to surrender as well.

And now the end is near. John is arrested. This voice from the wilderness who has troubled the comfortable is about to be silenced. The ultimate surrender is near at hand.

John is never so free as when he is behind bars. His work is complete. John is never so alive as when he is led to his execution. He is on the way to the bosom of Abraham.

And in this final surrender, never was John more the son of Elizabeth.

14

Samaritan Woman at Jacob's Well: Let's Talk

Racism renders people of color invisible. Sexism silences women. The despised race is not looked at; women are not listened to. Worse than children, the outcast is neither seen nor heard. Invisibility and silence are powerful ways to make powerless "the other." Little wonder those on the margin protest by turning to the media and shouting in society's collective face. They *will* be seen and heard.

Women are used to the silent treatment. Being interrupted becomes a way of life. There is a verbal yielding that is expected. Speech is limited to the telephone, over the back fence, and lunch at the club. A public voice about leading issues is reserved for others. Talk has its place. Speech is gender- and content-specific.

The story of the Samaritan woman at Jacob's well is remarkable for the place it affords a woman, a Samaritan woman, as a respected partner in dialogue. The story is profound for what it reveals about Jesus' relationship with women. The story is dangerous for how it challenges disciples of Jesus to see and speak with those considered to be "other."

In the modern office, the most interesting place to be is the water cooler. It is the shrine around which the faithful gather to discuss office politics and romantic interests and to handicap who is going to move up the corporate food chain. Likewise, the water wells in the Old Testament are the places to meet a wife: Abraham's servants find Rebecca, the future wife of Isaac, at the well of Nabor (Gen. 24:10f); Jacob meets Rachel at Haran (Gen. 29:1f); and Moses accepts Zipporah as his wife at the well in Midian (Ex. 2:16f). Jesus, the true Bridegroom who performed the first of his signs at the wedding at Cana, meets this Samaritan woman at Jacob's well. Jesus has come to "marry" Samaria (ancient Israel) so as to unite all of Israel in the new covenant of salvation. The encounter between Jesus and the

73

Samaritan woman is filled with marital images (fertility, marriage, water, well, vessel, and the like).

The Samaritan woman is without a name. However, this lack of personal identity signals her role as a representative figure for a particular group. She remains who she is, all the while transcending the limitations of individual identity. This Samaritan woman is at once "a she" and "a them" as well. Who is the Samaritan woman at the well?

She is the respected dialogue partner of Jesus! She is not a face, a set-up, or a straw figure for Jesus to teach a lesson. Even less is she an object of a moralizing message about too much marrying and not enough of a marriage. The Samaritan woman is without a name but not without a story. She has a voice. And most importantly, this Samaritan woman is blessed with a strong man who dares to speak *to* her. And she is wise enough to listen.

The conversation at Jacob's well between Jesus and the Samaritan woman is unique within the Fourth Gospel. Throughout John's Gospel, Jesus delivers extended monologues on critical topics (for example, the one with Nicodemus about being "born again"). Time and again, Jesus' dialogue partners soon drop out; the dialogue becomes a monologue. Not so with the woman at Jacob's well. The conversational character of the encounter abides. Jesus has found someone with whom he can give "living water," that is, his teaching or revelation from the Father, and disclose his own identity. It is a blessing to be understood. It is a gift to understand. Each gives and receives.

Conversation bespeaks intimacy. Women treasure being treated as respected partners in dialogue. The treasure is never more treasured by a woman than when the partner is insistent and the topic intensive.

Jesus enters into dialogue with the Samaritan woman about the deep down things of theology: worship, the Messiah, the covenant, history, and the mission to evangelize. At no point does the woman cease to be a respected partner in conversation. In the most shocking of ways, Jesus includes the Samaritan woman, and by extenuation, Samaria. Jesus' inclusion of the Samaritan woman is itself a sign of God's universal desire that all be saved. All the ancient (and current!) demons of exclusion—race, gender, religion, class—are exorcised.

Jesus returned to Galilee by way of Samaria. He stops at the most famous of wells: Jacob's. He finds a genuine partner for dialogue: a Samaritan woman. Jesus' encounter with this woman is a parable in action. It at once challenges a rigid world of meaning which is too comfortable for too few; it establishes a world of truth about the New Covenant of universal inclusion. Even the most hated and marginalized are called to be disciples.

Men treasure (though it is often buried beneath the bravado) being treated as respected partners in dialogue. Women give men permission to dream without seeming to be foolish. Women listen so as to invite men to give voice to their inner doubts without appearing to be weak. Women speak a truth which enables men to discover the truth about themselves.

Jesus reveals to the Samaritan woman the nature of true worship. He dares to dream and share what such a worship involves even in the face of a history of hostility between Samaritans and Jews. The reality of a divided community is acknowledged, "You people worship what you do not understand . . . salvation is from the Jews," says Jesus. At the same time there is a message of hope, "Yet an hour is coming and is now here when the real worshipers will worship the Father in Spirit and Truth." The woman responds to the issue of authentic worship by drawing Jesus out to the point that he reveals his divine identity: "I am he [the Messiah]."

The dialogue between Jesus and the Samaritan woman involves more than theory. Conversation leads to action. The woman left "her water jar and went back to the city." Like the disciples who left their fishing nets and daily occupations, this woman is an evangelizer. She goes to her Samaritan people with the message about Jesus. And the Fourth Gospel tells us, "many of the Samaritans . . . believed in him because of the woman's testimony." This woman's word of witness brings others to the Word made flesh. The Samaritans press Jesus to stay with them. He does, "and through his own word many more came to faith." The Samaritan woman—partner in dialogue, disciple, and evangelizer—does her part in establishing the New Covenant. At the end of the story the fruit of her work is revealed. The town comes to know the truth about Jesus, and can proclaim him to be "the Savior of the world."

The Fourth Gospel does not pretend the role of women in the Christian community is without tension. The disciples are shocked that Jesus is holding a conversation with a woman, and a Samaritan woman at that! Yet they do not enter into dialogue with Jesus. Unlike the woman, these disciples keep their reservations to themselves. The shocked (maybe even scandalized) disciples cannot bring themselves to ask, "Jesus, what do you want of this woman; a woman?"

The story of Jesus and the Samaritan woman is powerful, for it is a story that we do not study but ponder. A narrative that *interprets us* as we search its meaning. It is a shocking story that shakes the dust collected from unexamined premises which too often yield violent conclusions about "the others" (women, men, rich, poor, liberal, conservative). It is unsettling to be challenged to adopt an inclusive dialogue; listen to voices on the margins; and study portraits whose features are rarely detailed.

Above all, we must dare to ask what other disciples only thought: "Jesus, what do you want of this woman; a woman?"

Let the conversation commence.

15

Poor Widow: A Gift of Self

There is a close relationship between one's heart and one's treasure. For to learn about who we are, we must be aware of *what* we give, and *how*. Hence, it is not surprising that we find Jesus, who searches hearts and knows innermost thoughts, sitting at the temple treasury. It has been a long day of teaching, with more than its share of conflict and frustration. Jesus has been trying to convert hearts so as to change values. Jesus points the heart to that treasure which is beyond price, yet is there for *all* to receive. Yet the learned seek refuge in their intellect. The religious take comfort in the monuments to *their* righteousness.

What is Jesus to do? The day is long spent. So is the energy, even of the Teacher. As Jesus rises for the journey homeward, there is given to him (and to us) a teachable moment. Better yet, an occasion of grace. The eyes widen, yet focus on what is at hand. The energy gauge moves from *E* to *F*. The mind quickens and the heart beats faster still. Here in our midst is that union of heart and treasure revealing the value of a gift beyond its price.

We look with Jesus. What do we see? Before us is a *woman*. A *widow*. A widow who is *poor*. With all due respect to Jesus, we must wonder why the excitement. On any other occasion this poor widow would be invisible. We would not take note of her contribution. Yet here is Jesus drawing the attention of disciples and adversaries to her person, her gift, and her heart.

This poor widow is a person of quiet dignity and inner strength. She does not speak. Her eloquence comes from her presence, not from the abundance of her learning or accomplishments. We need not wrap her in our sentimental pity, nor ennoble her in our romantic piety. She meets obligations; accepts responsibility. She has something to give and will not be deterred by side glances, superior attitudes, or larger offerings.

The gift of this poor widow is two copper coins—all of a penny. Yet when we *risk* to look at this woman, we see her richness. The two coins tumble from a hand and heart both opened by generosity and abundance. There is no tight fist or shriveled heart. Her eyes reveal a soul that knows the blessings of giving, and in so doing, receiving a hundredfold.

A question lingers—why? And it is directed to the woman, not Jesus. *Why* have *you* put in all your living? Maybe she would rely on the kindness of strangers. Maybe she would become an object of charity (and in time the brunt of scorn).

Not so.

This is a case of those reasons which the mind knows not and only the heart understands.

The "why" of our question abides. We are offered no answer by Jesus. Our poor widow once again becomes invisible. She is covered over by those who rush to contribute their abundance. She must return to her everyday existence. There is no trace of a prince who will rescue or a glass slipper that turns rags to riches. Happily ever after is for fairy tales; blessedness flows from the Gospel. There is simply the enduring witness of this unknown woman who gave and gives yet again . . . to us.

And what does she give? What we most need—an example of that selflessness in which we really find ourselves. What is there left to come from this generous heart? Such a question bespeaks our relentless desire for more. What is left when our resources are spent are the gifts of the Spirit. Poverty of spirit yields a blessed heart bare of coins, so as to be fertile for the seeds of grace. What could possibly tumble from her hand outstretched? The stretching of the heart by the Spirit finds its way to an outstretched hand that yields to others and is wise enough to receive as a way of giving. The openness of heart and hand bespeaks that ebb and flow of gift that is at once given and received.

There is a hand that remains pressed to the heart, its contents hidden from view. There is about life a mystery which we do not see. There is a Providence which counts the hairs of our head, and is never outdone in generosity.

When the coins of our lives are offered, there is a risk to be sure. We can be rejected, taken for granted, or simply ignored. Yet the true gift by a generous heart and open hand never calculates the return. Gifts given take on a life of their own. When our poor efforts have spent their power, amazing grace makes up what is lacking.

So let us not look at the coins of others. Let us not judge by the standards of abundance. Rather, let us be mighty with *our* little coins. For if we proceed from the generous heart, we give the true gift—ourselves!

16

Herodias and Salome:
My Daughter; Myself

Culture wars over the arts is nothing new. Plato wanted to banish the poets in his utopian Republic. The popes sought to direct the arts by controlling the artists. Today we witness ideological battles over the place, function, and funding of the arts in a democratic society. A common thread runs throughout: the arts unleash and express powerful forces within human natures for human culture. The arts are never simply about entertainment. The arts interface with morals. The arts reveal and conceal our deepest hopes and repressed fears.

The ancients accorded a special place to the power of dance, especially ritual dance. Such a performance prepared the people for a sacrifice . . . human or otherwise! Hence, dance is dangerous. Dance contains varying degrees of death. The body human speaks a language-in-motion about the power of seduction, the fear of conquest, and the sacrifice of the victim. The ebb and flow, opening and closing, the bodily burst of Eros and the frozen stillness of Thanatos arouse the passions and evoke the imagination. In dance, body and soul join as one and the audience becomes one with the performer. To dance is to unite the audience for the sacrifice. The audience participates, through the dancer, in the killing of the innocent victim. Yet individual responsibility and guilt are diffused throughout the crowd. Everyone participates but no *one* is guilty or responsible for the shedding of innocent blood.

John the Baptist's beheading attests to the deadly power of dance. And Herodias is masterful at choreographing this mortal moment. Salome, daughter to the mother, dances her part to lethal perfection. John is but another instance of the fate which awaits the authentic prophet of the Lord by a crowd gone murderous. His death is linked backward to the spilled blood of Abel, and forward to that blood of the Innocent Lamb who takes away the sins of the world. But the shedding of the innocent blood of the Suffering Servant lies sometime in the future. For now our focus is on the royal palace of Herod. The sound of music, mixed with gay laughter, belies the deadly turn the festivities are about to take.

John has long been a burr under the throne of Herod and Herodias. John spoke truth to power: "It is not lawful for you to have your brother's wife." Not even the king is above God's moral law. This reminder engendered resentment by Herodias, once married to Philip, the brother of Herod. Resentment matured into a grudge, the common reaction to moral correction. The smoldering ember of a grudge waits its chance to flare into the consuming flame of vengeance. The moment is at hand.

And what better moment to mask murder than at a party. Herod throws a birthday celebration—for himself! How in character. The wine is flowing, the inhibitions are lowered, and the entertainment is intoxicating the senses. It is a time of maximum venerability and minimum prudence. The festivities have reached a fever pitch. It is time for Herodias to strike the match that lights the flames of a resentment which kills.

Enter Salome; the daughter and the dance. The "John problem" is about to be solved. Herod, intoxicated by wine and with himself, is delighted by the dance. His respect, admiration, and fear of John are washed down by wine and the seduction of Salome. Herod is helpless. The dance has disarmed the king and prepared the crowd for the sacrifice of innocent blood. Herodias's behind the scenes manipulation of situation and daughter yields its fruit. Herod says to Salome: " 'Ask me for whatever you wish, and I will grant it.' And he vowed to her, 'Whatever you ask me, I will give to you, even half of my kingdom.' " The celebration of self reaches a fever pitch. There is no limit to what Herod will give. However, his generosity is really pomposity. The grandiose will satisfy the grudge. Herodias's deadly deliverence is but a request away.

Daughter seeks mother. Reflection finds mirror. The question that binds: "Mother, what shall I ask for?" This is the enduring inquiry of daughter to mother: "What to be? Do? Seek?" Success. Fame. Popularity. Desirability. Virtue. Nobility. The litany is endless. The influence of mother on daughter is ongoing. Mother gives birth twice to each daughter: the nativity of nature and the abiding birth of character.

For Herodias the dance lessons for Salome are about to pay dividends. The dutiful daughter turns to the manipulative mother: "What shall I ask?" The delight of Herodias can hardly be contained. Victory is at hand. "The head of John the baptizer," is the trophy demanded which signals the triumph of Herodias over her nemesis. Salome rushes to Herod with her (mother's) demand: "I want you to give me at once the head of John the Baptist on a platter." The fevered frenzy of the moment must be seized.

Passions must not be allowed to cool. Emotions must cloud reason. The wine of pride must not wear off. The intoxicated Herod must fulfill his vow "at once."

Sobering thoughts begin to emerge within a somber Herod. The mood swings in dramatic fashion. Things have gotten out of hand. Yet face saving must be achieved at the cost of the loss of innocent life. The power of the dance has turned the celebrants into a crowd on the way to being a mob. The instability of a group without a leader bespeaks danger. Herod will not stand up to Herodias. He is not about to stand for John against a bloodthirsty crowd finetuned by Salome's dance. Violence is contagious. Herod and the crowd become one in sacrificing the innocent. The end is never in doubt.

Salome receives the head of John and passes the prize to Herodias. She has been taught what to ask for. She has learned the lesson well. Their partnership has proved to be highly efficient. There is no trace of inter-generational conflict. The innocent blood of John has joined the genera-tions: mother and daughter, parent and child, beautiful seductress and mature manipulator, together bewitching the king and silencing the prophet.

We don't know what becomes of Herodias and Salome. But it is not beyond the reach of reason to postulate the following: violence is genera-tional. Violence begets violence. Abuse obeys the laws of inertia: once in motion an inner dynamic completes the cycle. Battered parents are bat-tered children who batter children. Spouses who abuse spouses have been schooled in domestic violence. Hence, there may be a day when the future daughter of Salome inquires of her: "What shall I ask?" The mother lives in the daughter and echoes a voice long past, arriving anew. Prologue is prelude. Yesteryear becomes yester-now. "Mother, what shall I ask?" taunts Salome and haunts Herodias. For in the question of this yet-to-be daugh-ter/granddaughter, the blood of John is spilled again.

The Gospel does not end with the beheading of John and his burial by disciples. Such would be a resolution of despair. Rather, the Gospel is a revolution of hope. Herodias and Salome must give way to those women under the Cross, those women who came to anoint the body of the One dead who now lives!

The One who is Lord of the dance of life.

What will *you* ask?

17

Woman Caught in Adultery: The Rest of the Story

"**I** need to tell you something," said Gomer as she rushed into the home of Leah.

"Slow down," responded Leah as she made her way to the kitchen table. "Are the elders or the Romans after you?" continued Leah with a slight laugh. Leah and Gomer had been friends for the past three years. They met when Leah moved, with her son, from a neighboring village. Unfortunately, Leah's husband had died and she is raising Mosha by herself.

"I don't know how to say this," began Gomer as she found a chair, while searching for the words (not to mention the courage) to continue.

"I've had relations with another man." As the words poured out so did the tears.

"I didn't mean for this to happen," said Gomer, "it just happened. I don't know what to do."

Leah sat frozen, her eyes fixed on Gomer whose head was downcast as she emitted sounds of sobbing.

Leah's look was not one of judgment but of recognition. There was a connection of person to person, woman to woman, and . . .

"I can't believe I got into this situation," said Gomer after gaining her composure. "It just doesn't make sense."

Leah had to regain her wits as well.

"I certainly didn't expect to hear this," said Leah. "I thought you and Aaron were making a go of things."

"You know how Aaron can be," countered Gomer. "He can be so coarse at times. There is no tenderness or love. Besides, he's so caught up with his family. I might as well not exist, except when he wants a release. I bet he has taken others."

The sobbing of Gomer ceased and was replaced with a defensive edge.

Gomer was now standing and pacing the floor.

Leah remained seated and silent. "Don't you have anything to say?" said Gomer as if Leah was the guilty party. "I hope you're not judging me. I took a big chance in telling you this."

Leah finally shook free of her mental cobwebs to once again wake in the present. "I am not your judge," began Leah. "I committed my share of sins. You don't need a judge. You need a friend."

"I knew you would understand," said Gomer as she found her seat once again. Her eyes managed to find those of Leah.

"What do you think I should do?" said Gomer, hoping to find some quick way out of this potentially deadly situation.

Leah was once again in her private world of yesteryear. The dusty corners of her memory kept giving up their secrets. The past is never past. Issues long settled resurface to disturb the peace.

"Leah, what should I do?!" repeated Gomer with a mixture of urgency and impatience. "I don't know how much longer I can keep hiding all this from Aaron."

"First you need to stop hiding from yourself," said Leah with a blunt honesty that made Gomer think she had made *another* mistake.

"I thought you weren't going to judge me," Gomer shot back. "You said I needed a friend, not a judge."

"That's what I am being, Gomer," responded Leah. "I'm the kind of friend who's going to tell you the truth . . . at least the truth as I see it."

"And what do you see?" snapped Gomer.

"I see a person who is very afraid," said Leah, "and someone who is fearful of taking responsibility."

"Of course I'm afraid," said Gomer. "Do you have any idea where all this could lead? I mean I don't relish the thought of the . . . well, you know." Gomer's voice trailed off. Just completing the thought is too much to ask.

"I kind of have an idea what you're going through," said Leah, "and you must face yourself and what you have done. There is no living with infidelity."

"I don't know what you mean," said Gomer in a whine, which only serves to irritate Leah.

"I mean you have to see that none of this *just* happened. *You* caused it! *You* went with this other man. *You* made the decision to break your vows," said Leah with an earnestness that revealed compassion, not condemnation.

"You can't live with yourself or anybody else," continued Leah, "without acknowledging what you did."

"But you know how Aaron can be," objected Gomer. "He can be so . . ." Gomer never finished her sentence.

"Stop it!" said Leah with obvious anger. "Don't blame Aaron, or circumstances, or the other guy you went with. You haven't been honest with Aaron. You're not being honest with me or yourself."

With that burst of moral passion, words ceased and their eyes met and became as one. It was as if each woman looked into the soul of the other and saw her own reflection.

Slowly their eyes turned down and inward. There is only so much truth we can bear.

Both women allowed their fingers to roam at will over the table. It was as if they were writing or painting what they would say or do next.

Finally Leah broke the silence.

"Look," Leah said as she tried a smile while looking at her fingers, "you don't have to be afraid with me. I'd be the last one to condemn you. It's just that if you don't do it now, it only becomes harder. The deception becomes more deadly."

It was Gomer's turn to break the silence.

"I've never had to face myself before," said Gomer in a voice at once calm but intense. "No one ever loved me enough to risk the truth. Maybe others did love me in that way but I just didn't see it."

"It's not always easy to face who and what you are," said Leah. "This is especially true when others take delight in our failures."

"Or others use our failures to elevate themselves," added Gomer. "But you're right, I brought about this situation. I want to try and make things right."

"And you can," said Leah as she touched the hand of Gomer. "Worse than accepting responsibility is becoming a self-pitying victim."

"I guess I'm back at the beginning," said Gomer with an air of determination and strength. "I need some guidance in terms of action."

"Go back to Aaron and don't ever see the other man again," said Leah. "You can't turn back the clock, but you can make a new start now. You can make your marriage work."

"But you said there is no living with infidelity," objected Gomer.

"That's right," said Leah, "as long as you don't face yourself and accept responsibility. However, the past doesn't have to cripple your future. Just go and get on with your life. But only you can do that."

"It won't be easy," said Gomer, welling up in heart and eyes, "but I know you're right. I am so glad I talked to you. I love you."

"I love you too," said Leah.

The two women embraced. Gomer left to start the long journey homeward.

No sooner had the door closed than a small, handsome bundle of energy burst into the solitude. "Mom, I'm starving." Life goes on.

18

Woman with a Hemorrhage:
Reach Out and Touch

The well positioned know what they want and how to get it. A case in point is Jarius, one of the rulers of the synagogue. He is a man of influence and reputation. He has a name and a need. Jarius's "little daughter is at the point of death." Jarius, a leader of the synagogue, turns to Jesus, the itinerate preacher. Desperate situations call for desperate action: "Come and lay your hand on her, so that she may be well, and live." Off Jesus goes, accompanied by a "large crowd," the result of Jarius's position, Jesus' reputation, and the dire need of the daughter. Drama draws a crowd.

Numbered among the crowd is a woman with a need as well. She has suffered from "a flow of blood for twelve years." Compounding her complaint is the years of being subjected to needless medical treatment. All of her money has been spent on cures that do not heal. Furthermore, she is poorly positioned to gain access and a hearing before Jesus. She is but one among many, and by no means an important one. She has no name, no synagogue, and no status. Yet these obstacles will not ultimately obstruct. Desperate situations call for determined action. She will risk a reach to *touch* Jesus.

Why Jesus? The answer is clear: "She has heard reports about Jesus." There is more at work here than a typical woman trafficking in gossip. The reports about Jesus' reputation as a healer have made the rounds. Those on the bottom and at the margins suffer a deficiency of income and information. They are susceptible to the quick-fix quackery of the day. Their money is spent on the futile. Fragments of information often fragment life as a whole. They must pick up bits and pieces. The scraps that fall from the lectern of the learned are tossed to the outsider. Easy manipulation comes through fragmentation. The whole story is seldom told to those on the fringe. Knowledge is power. Withholding a piece of the puzzle keeps the powerless dependent.

The woman approaches Jesus *from behind*. A frontal approach is for the assured. She makes her way from the rear. She is used to living in the back and being pushed to the side. She will not risk a verbal exchange. Such belongs to those with the power of words and the position to speak. She must settle for a touch of his garment. Is this not a revelation of her superstition? Do we not see magic being masked as faith? Is not touching his garment akin to fingering the rabbit's foot or clutching the lucky bean?

No doubt there is something of the magical at work; a faith less than pristine. Yet the ideal should not be the enemy of the real. What *can* be should build upon what is. But there is more at work than a desperate woman in the grip of mere magic. She is *ritually* unclean. The flow of blood, for whatever reason, makes her "unclean." By extension, anyone touched by the one who is unclean becomes unclean as well. In respecting the requirements from Leviticus (15:19-31), she refrains from touching Jesus. In not touching Jesus, she preserves *his* purity! In addition, her refusal to directly request a healing is born of years of scorn and shame. She has suffered this flow of blood for the past twelve years. She has suffered at the hands of failed medicine. Deeper still have been the slings and arrows of those who flee in order to remain "clean," the judgments of intimates who cannot comprehend the malady. To risk humiliation by *this* healer would be too much. Hence, a touch of his garment, under the cover of the crowd, might just be enough.

So it is. "And immediately the hemorrhage ceased; and she felt in her body that she was healed of her disease." The mere touch of Jesus' garment accomplished what all the physicians had been unable to achieve. The healing was not in her mind but in her body. She *knew* she was healed, and who it was who brought about her relief. The cure was immediate and direct. This was no momentary episode of mind over infirmity, only to return when the charismatic healer moves on. She was healed.

As the woman feels her healing, Jesus perceives "that power had gone forth from him." True healing calls for courage and costly grace. The woman had the courage to touch Jesus' garment. The healing of this woman took something out of Jesus. Authentic healing comes at a price. When Jesus heals he always gives something of himself. Jesus does more than merely prescribe medicines, herbs, and treatments. Jesus is always involved with the one who comes to him, even one who dares to touch his garment. There is no impersonal, technical transaction between provider and consumer. Healing is person to person. Risk meets response. Touch drains power. Healer needs renewal.

And renewal comes with Jesus meeting the woman now healed. Jesus *must* know who touched him, who received his power, who has been made whole. The one cured is not to be counted among the rich and famous, the movers and shakers. She is not one of the well positioned but approaches from behind and just touches his garment. She hoped to touch, to be cured, and to be gone without notice. Just another anonymous face in the crowd. Not so.

The woman comes forward "in fear and trembling." No more coming from behind. The cover of the crowd has been blown. She is now face to face with the one whose garment she touched, and in whom his power has gone. Before Jesus, she tells "him the whole truth." Will he now take back his power? Will her infirmity return? Will she be made an object of scorn? Worse, will she be condemned as "unclean" and one who made others unclean?

None of the above. The one who tells the whole truth, to the One who is Truth, is set free. "Daughter, your faith has made you well; go in peace, and be healed of your disease." This woman is now a "daughter" and not merely an episode of the healing ministry. There is an affection which transcends the affection. The relationship between Jesus and this woman-daughter is now one of a mature faith. She is to no longer approach Jesus from the rear and touch of his garments. The voice of truth and the victory of faith now empower her to speak *with* Jesus. The healing of the hemorrhage has given way to a deeper healing: a well-being of the soul. She is now clean beyond the ritual requirements in Leviticus. She is now to be counted among the pure of heart. Anxiety is to give way to peace. To be healed is to go forward and live the gift. As for Jesus, the daughter of Jarius awaits.

The woman with the twelve-year flow of blood became the woman healed, and eventually a daughter-in-faith of Jesus, because she risked reaching out to touch. The unclean became clean. We all suffer some form of uncleanliness. We have tried all the modern methods of "medicine," both physical and spiritual. Yet our disease remains. We continue to search for that faith which yields that peace beyond price. This woman teaches that such is ours if we but approach Jesus with "the whole truth" of our lives. There is no need for fear and trembling. Our whole truth is always received by Jesus' total love.

And it is love which drives out all fear.

19

Martha and Mary: Sisters

Life on the road is rough. Even for an iterate preacher of the Kingdom who also just happens to be the Messiah. For this is the Son of Man who has not a place to lay his head. The open road has come to own the son of a carpenter with roots in Bethlehem and Nazareth. This son of Mary continues to be about his Father's business.

Yet even the Messiah needs some "r and r"—rest and relaxation. Jesus turns to the kindness of strangers and the company of women; a pair of sisters to be exact: Martha and Mary. Drawing on a special source of material, Luke provides us with an intimate moment in the life of Jesus and two of his benefactors (disciples).

Jesus likes women. He respects them, is at home with them in their home, and acknowledges their dignity in ways that are rare for that time and place. To extend hospitality is the gift of self. To open one's home to another is to open one's heart to receive the gift that is each guest. Martha and Mary have opened their homes and hearts to Jesus.

It is one thing to extend an invitation; it is another to meet the requirements of hospitality. Martha receives Jesus, and it falls to her to make her house a home. As we enter we are introduced to Mary, Martha's sister. She is sitting "at the Lord's feet and listening to his teaching." It is a thoroughly human moment: a young woman in the presence of a strong young man of danger. And this man is speaking to her mind and touching her heart. The teaching of Jesus is not for the elite few, but for all who are able to listen, for when Jesus teaches there is more involved than words or doctrines. Jesus offers himself to each disciple. One does not listen to Jesus without being affected. There is an authority which separates Jesus from all other teachers. Mary is mesmerized by the intensity of the encounter.

Jesus is also enjoying the company of this attentive young woman.

There have been times when his preaching has been met with less than attentive appreciation. Some have even picked up stones to silence the preacher. Yet here is a young woman at Jesus' feet; hungering for his words. She is a disciple.

Jesus did not come to Martha's house to conduct a class. He came for hospitality. That is Martha's perspective, and it is one not shared by Mary. Martha is caught up in the devilish details of hospitality. No doubt Martha wants to make a good impression. She wants to do the right thing. An elaborate meal, one with many dishes, is being prepared. More hands and less listening would be appreciated. Since no one seems mindful of Martha's plight, it is time for a not so gentle lesson of her own. Well, more of a complaint; and it is directed to Jesus: "Lord, do you not care that my sister has left me to serve alone? Tell her then to help me." It is a thoroughly human complaint. Martha's project is beyond her resources. There is a loss of proportion which Martha tries to right by involving others, namely, Jesus and Mary.

Jesus will not be drawn into a sisterly squabble. Discretion is the better part of valor—even for the Lord! Jesus offers Martha some perspective without being pejorative. Jesus needs and welcomes hospitality. Yet it should be a respite from the anxious, troubling world, not more of the same. The details have become ends rather than means to authentic hospitality; the meal has become more important than the guest. Domestic tranquillity has given way to performance anxiety. The swirl around Martha is threatening to draw everyone into its turbulence. Jesus values the hospitality but he loves Martha and Mary. And he would love them even if they had no home to offer, hospitality to extend, or meal to prepare. Jesus accepted the invitation because of Martha and not all the details of hospitality.

At no time does Jesus denounce Martha. Mary can listen and Jesus can teach because food is on the way. Jesus is not writing Mary a blank check to feel superior or boast about "her portion." Each sister has chosen a portion. Each portion has its benefits and burdens. The portion Martha has chosen has produced anxiety, trouble, and distraction. All of this results because something which passes—a hospitable meal—has been treated as if it is ultimate and absolute. That's the way it is with the things of this world that are treated as if they were the things of heaven. High anxiety results when we select portions which are too *small*. We resent what others have. We want them to give up their portion and share our anxiety. Misery loves company. Anxiety needs a companion. Jesus refuses to arbitrate the dispute in favor of Martha. Mary is not to relinquish what she has chosen.

This brief episode in the life of Jesus has been the favorite of preachers down through the ages. Unfortunately a wedge has been forged where none was intended. Over time Martha and Mary came to represent all manner of things theological and spiritual. The result has been an incomplete either/or rather than a mature both/and. Martha has been sullied by association: pragmatic, compulsive, utilitarian, and a model of achiever fever. Mary has been saluted as a model of authentic discipleship. Which model should mold? Easy. Mary. Which portion for our daily bread? A snap. Mary.

None of this is intended by the story. The spiritual life of the disciples and the community of disciples called church require *both* for following Jesus. Mary's portion, though honored by Jesus, runs the risk of being distorted. If *all* Mary does is sit at Jesus' feet and listen, a pietistic passivity creeps in. Listening must lead to living the word that is heard. Martha's portion runs the obvious risk of becoming a frantic activism without a foundation in Jesus' word. It is a good humanism to be sure, but it is secular more than spiritual. Martha embodies the result: anxiety, resentment, fatigue, and a distraction from the things that really matter. Yet when the portions are blended we gain a portrait that captures the fullness of discipleship. The whole emerges from the details, rich in texture and truth.

The favorable rating of Mary in recent times has been on the ascent. Martha has once again "headed south" in the polls. Much of this is generational. The "forty-somethings" have embraced the Martha portion of the American pie: MBA, BMW, and a weekly visit to the shrink concerning that hollow feeling within. It's time for the Mary portion with its invitation to sit, listen, and meditate about deep down things. Martha in modern dress, the yuppie type, has been blamed for all manner of maladies: pollution, materialism, and the break up of the family. Mary is adorned in simple dress; no designer garb for her. She is adored as the ideal for a generation burned out on acquiring the symbols of success.

Before we too quickly take sides, the Fourth Gospel adds a muddling stroke to trouble the Martha-Mary portrait. Lazarus, the brother of these sisters, has died. Jesus delayed his coming, and Martha is more confrontational than complaining. (Not surprising, Mary must be summoned from home to the tomb.) Martha is unhappy twice over: her brother is dead and Jesus dilly-dallied around the Jordan. Jesus tries to talk the "theology of hope" but Martha isn't listening. She wants her brother and an explanation. She gets both in the *person* of Jesus. "I am the resurrection and the Life."

The active, confrontational Martha receives what she has needed all along: Jesus. Not Jesus as a guest or a theological teacher but as a *person;* the Word made flesh. And through this encounter with the person of Jesus, Martha echoes Peter's profession of faith: "Yes Lord; I believe that you are the Christ, the Son of God, he who is coming into the world."

Martha has come to choose the better portion. *Jesus* shall not be taken from her.

20

Mother of James and John: Blind Ambition

Mark and Matthew provide us with a story about two brothers and a mother locked in blind ambition. At first blush the story seems to be a clear case of "the climbing disease" which infects members of organizations, especially hierarchies. Yet on closer inspection there is lurking a distinction in the stories which highlights a deep difference. The variation on the theme of ambition revolves around the *who* and not the what. For the one(s) who make the request of Jesus differ in Mark and Matthew.

The more primitive story belongs to Mark. In his version it is the two disciples, James and John, who request the positions of power. In the Matthean version it is the ambitious mother who requests of Jesus the places of honor for her sons. Naturally we want to know—why? Why does Matthew feel the need to insert an ambitious mother?

We should avoid all the Freudian temptations to psychologize the episode. We simply don't know if the writer of Matthew had a "mother's complex." We simply don't know if James and John's mother was a driven, compulsive woman living through her children. What we do know is that the account in Mark is older and closer to the historical episode. The two brothers approached Jesus with the request for positions of importance. Mark's Gospel is never one to hide a flaw or expose a foible of the human condition. Even heroes have flaws. Blemishes are acknowledged as simply a part of the human condition. Hence, the disciples could be faithful to Jesus *and* still be ambitious. Mark reports that the other ten disciples become indignant. The ambition bug stings and spreads its fever among the faithful. "We want a throne too!" Oh boy.

Matthew's Gospel is later and more "respectful" of the dignity of the disciples. The distance of time and space lends enchantment and the need to polish the image. The defects in our role models must be kept from view lest we

97

become scandalized and lose faith. Over time there is a need felt to school present and future generations in the ways of virtue. Hence, the bug of ambition, the sting of vice, must be covered over.

What better way to take the moral heat off James and John than by introducing an ambitious mother. All the stereotypical images of a Jewish mother come to the fore: anxious, ambitious, and living vicariously through her sons. Matthew's Jewish mother is the perfect deflector for our disciples. Mother made them seek it!

The interjection of a woman to blame is not new and ought not surprise. Women have taken the fall for men quite often. Mothers often step in the way of life's arrows directed at their children. Mothers push, prod, and parade their children before various audiences, apperative and otherwise. It's the motherly thing to want Elizabeth to dazzle with dance and Stephanie to sing that song, and the world stills to listen. Mothers want daughters to date and sons to be athletic gentlemen. Every son and daughter is but a nudge away from the crown of Miss America and football immortality with the Heisman Trophy.

Yet most mothers "settle" for the real and hope for the best. A beautiful wedding photo and the high school football letter jacket acquire a value beyond price. More importantly, mothers want a daughter blessed with a happy home and a son who has become a man in the best sense.

Mothers start their "second careers" as they parent a new generation in need of a "little coaxing." Another chance to get it right. Another blessing from above. This time the pressure's off. Nothing to prove. No one to live through. A someone to live for. A love to love with that comes without the strings of full accountability. A love to shower that makes all new and each heart young again. A hope in lives formed over time which allows one to die at peace. All is safe; each is protected.

A prudent approach to prayer is always in season. We need to be careful what we pray for; we might get it! Too often our prayer is an endless list of wants masking as needs for the good of the soul. However, on closer inspection, they are our cravings for ease, honor, or some temporal achievement. How often have we stormed heaven with our list, only to be disappointed with the acquisition. The date is a dud. The job turns out to be a dead end. The acceptance letter fills us with a pride that heads us toward a fall. We prayed. We received. We're disappointed.

The ambition of the mother of James and John drives her to rash prayer. Fellowship with Jesus requires sharing his cup before one can share his crown, for the cup is one of suffering and leads to the cross. The crown of glory is fashioned with thorns, not fine gold. Each true disciple of Jesus must make cup and crown his own. Yet ambition blinds the eye to the unpleasant. Authentic achievement requires more than ambition or the desire for glory. There are crosses which test character, obstacles which try one's soul, and setbacks which strengthen one's resolve. Mother sees only the finished product and not the refining process. The moment of glory overshadows the long and winding road. The acceptance into glory calls for an apprenticeship in suffering.

Jesus understands the desires of a mother for her sons. He has a Jewish mother as well! Hence, he forces the sons to come from behind their mother's dress: "Are you able to drink the cup that I am to drink?" They respond with echoes of a mother's influence. "We are able." So be it. James and John will drink the cup of martyrdom and so share in Jesus' destiny and glory. However, seats of special honor are assigned by the Father. It is sufficient to share the cup of Jesus.

To drink the cup of Jesus is not self-indulgent gulping, but a lifelong self-emptying through the daily sipping of serving others. The cup of Jesus is filled with a different brew than the mixture offered by the world. For the cup of glory of the world is pressed to the lips and fills one with the promise of power. The cup of service to Jesus is pressed to the heart, so one is poured out for others in love. The cup of the world freely offers its seats of honor to the high and the mighty. Yet in time the brew becomes bitter and the seats must be quickly relinquished for the new movers and shakers. The cup of Jesus cannot be served before its time. There is a schooling of the heart required before drinking *this* cup. It is the school of humility, daily heroism, off camera sacrifice, and that quiet courage which wins the hour for light over darkness, love over fear, and that good and right which triumphs over wickedness.

The cup of Jesus is offered to each mother—yes, even the mother of James and John. Granted, her ambition is extreme. Her request is for a misplaced glory. Yet she brings her sons to Jesus. Her influence allows them to accept the cup of Jesus and share in his baptism of fire. All of this is possible because at some level the mother of James and John drank the cup of Jesus.

Jesus acknowledges the request. He accepts her sons. They will follow the Lord to Jerusalem and all which that implies. And what about this ambitious mother? What is to become of her? Matthew, who introduces her into this story of ambition, supplies the answer. As Jesus breathes his last on Golgotha, a group of women who ministered to him as he ministered to others "look on from afar." And numbered among these faithful disciples is "the mother of the sons of Zebedee" (Mt 27:55-56).

The ambitious mother is also the good mother and a faithful disciple. She drinks from the same cup as her sons. Just maybe one of those seats next to Jesus is reserved for . . .

21

Woman Who Anoints Jesus: Waste Not, Love Not

One person's generosity is another's extravagance. The difference is detected through the motivation. The *why* uncovers the *which*. Generosity is the giving of self for the good of the other. Extravagance is the giving of things for the praise of self. Generosity enriches the giver and encourages the receiver to be generous when able. Extravagance impoverishes the giver and demeans the receiver. Generosity overcomes greed. Extravagance is greed in appealing costume. Grasping hands, wide eyes, and narrow heart are masked by the flow of things and the rush of abundance. Such a show is a trap to ensnare the prey; it is domination of the other and elevation of the self.

The extravagant denounce the generous in the name of *waste*. Such is the plight of the woman who anoints Jesus. It must be admitted that we don't deal well with generosity. The little voice of suspicion repeats its prudent mantra: "Beware. Never something for nothing. Too much. Back off." Even the gospels have trouble with this "anointing woman." But her generosity evokes a like generosity in Jesus, for he declares her act will be forever associated with the preaching of the Gospel. Yet while the act abides, her name does not. There is a wide divergence in details as well. There is no conspiracy to get the story straight. However, a gem of generosity is present, and Jesus promises it will be preserved and proclaimed until he comes again. The remembrance is of *her*. Hence, her portrait is required painting. Her action requires repeating.

From the gospels emerge three faces of the anointing woman: an anonymous one with an alabaster jar, a woman of ill repute, and Mary, the sister of Martha and Lazarus. Of course these three cannot be one and the same. What abides, however, is the *act* of anointing by one who does not speak. What emerges is a shocking picture of God revealed in the portrait of this woman (these women): a woman who knows the value more than the price; the cost more than the expense.

What this woman does is "waste" herself in service to Jesus. For the time is coming when Jesus will "waste" himself on the Cross. The anointing woman, unnamed and silent, invades a male-only dinner at the house of Simon the leper. The reaction is typical: anger. The rationalization is predictable: "this ointment could have been sold for a large sum, and the money given to the poor." (How rich the poor would be if they received even a small portion of all the good intentions!) Of course the poor are not the concern. The woman's generosity is distorted as "waste" by the disciples who are more fearful than resentful. And their fear is about death.

Throughout Jesus' ministry the disciples have tried to discourage him from journeying to Jerusalem. Peter has been most vocal in "protecting" Jesus from his baptism of fire and cup of suffering. Yet Jesus has rebuked Peter for speaking the words of Satan. Jesus must go to Jerusalem, be rejected, suffer, and die, so that sins will be forgiven. Jesus can only rise *after* he suffers and dies. The disciples simply cannot face Jesus' death. They also know that they will share the fate of Jesus in Jerusalem. They must face rejection as well as their own mortality. When this woman anoints the body of Jesus she challenges their denial of death. Her action of "waste" occasions Jesus to once again teach about his messiahship and the cost of discipleship: "By pouring this ointment on my body she has prepared me for burial." The Gospels of Matthew and John are in agreement on this point: the anointment is revelatory of Jesus' death. To be a disciple is to be anointed for burial as well! This woman's waste is a prophetic act which troubles their comfortable denial.

Luke's account of the anointing takes a somewhat different slant in terms of the woman's identity. She is a woman of ill repute. This designation fits perfectly with Luke's theology. Namely, Luke highlights the mercy and forgiveness of God made visible in the person and ministry of Jesus. Jesus is the Compassion of God who calls the lost sheep and prodigal children back to the Father. The woman who anoints Jesus' feet, bathes them in her tears, and dries them with her hair is proclaimed "forgiven her many sins." More importantly, "she has shown great love." She can love so much because she has been so completely forgiven her sins. This woman can "waste" all that ointment and tears because she is loved and forgiven. Her anointing of Jesus bespeaks his death. Her washing with tears bespeaks the forgiveness of sins. In her anointing and washing, a shocking portrait of God begins to take shape on a canvas not always to our liking.

This anointing woman, whose act is to be forever remembered, is a woman of waste. She reveals the Messiah who must suffer and die. She reveals the God who loves sinners in a special way. Simply put, this wasteful woman incarnates the Wasteful God!

In Luke's account Jesus is in the home of Simon the Pharisee for table fellowship. Our woman of ill repute, the woman of anointing and washing, provides an occasion for the Pharisee to pass judgment, more on Jesus than on the woman: "If this man were a prophet, he would have known who and what kind of woman this is who is touching him—that she is a sinner." Revealed in these words is Simon's portrait of God. And his God is too small. For the God of Simon is exacting, righteous, lawful, just, demanding, and one worthy of our respect—and fear. Alas, this small God is devoid of mercy and compassion. The God of Simon would never "waste" himself on creatures small and sinful. Such a God would never move us to weep tears of joy at having been forgiven. Even less would such a small God move us to forgive another or to forgive ourselves.

The God of the anointing woman is a God who wastes himself on us. She reveals a God who is passionately, madly in love with us. Such a God throws reserve, respectability, and reverence away in favor of involvement with his children, great and small. The God who wastes himself on Golgotha reveals the depth of his commitment and care. Rational calculation, questions of merit, and evaluation of moral worth are all set aside in a show of unbounded, wasteful love upon love. The waste of Good Friday blends into the risen life that is Easter morn.

Every great expression of love involves a great waste according to the canons of reason and calculations of cost-benefit analysis. Yet love transcends the bottom line and the line of inquiry which demands to know, "What's in it for me?" Great loves cannot be crunched by numbers or comprehended by the computer. Love has its reasons which pure utility knows not.

Justify, in terms of budget and energy, keeping company with the sick friend and handicapped child; the slow student and the son with AIDS; the terminal patient and the Alzheimer's parent. Endless is the list of ways we waste with love, the anointings we administer with oil and tear to signify our love beyond measure. While our pockets may be empty, our hearts are full. The bread is sliced thinner; the love is cut thicker.

Love not.
Waste not.
Know not
The God who
spares not
His Son
for you.

22

Mary Magdalene:
Second Chances

$\mathfrak{G}$reat biblical drama often occurs in less than grand settings. The birth of the Messiah is in a stable. The props shouldn't obstruct the message and the messenger. The scenery is secondary; the proclamation primary. The starkness of stage serves to highlight the abundance of grace and truth.

The drama of salvation draws us onto a hill. We pass to a borrowed tomb. And now we find ourselves in a garden, a garden filled with the familiar and lush with mystery. The garden of our fall has become the garden of our resurrection. The grasp of pride has been replaced with the emptying of humble service. The Adam and Eve have given way to the Magdala and the Messiah of Easter morn. The journey is no longer backward to a Paradise Lost, but forward to a Kingdom found in spirit and truth.

The simple setting of the garden focuses our attention on Mary and Jesus.

Mary of Magdala is a remarkable woman. She is found at the tomb of the One who was crucified through the unholy alliance of religion and politics: synagogue and Governor's house. Jesus' capital punishment was meant to be public and serve as a lesson to all who refuse to render unto Caesar. His cross awaits those who desire the glory of the Father more than the human praise. The scattered must remain scattered. There will be no public display of support. Sorrow will be behind closed doors and within hearts. No more talk of the Messiah. The crowd is not to be excited with the hope of deliverance. Supporters are to be kept away. Only those who drive nails and guard the tomb risk standing beneath the cross.

Yet we know present on *that* hill, keeping company with the convicted, is Mary of Magdala. Out of love she risks being numbered among his sympathizers. She is willing to risk a similar fate rather than abandon the One who did not abandon her. Mary of Magdala, guilty but made whole by Jesus, is found with the One who is innocent but judged guilty. Furthermore, she is not content to risk arrest on Good Friday. Mary comes to the tomb "early on the first day of the week." Another act of civil disobedience from this woman who loves much because she has been forgiven much.

In the darkness of that "first day" emerges the figure of a woman approaching the tomb of Jesus of Nazareth. She comes into the darkness not out of fear, but out of eagerness to minister to the One who ministered to her. Upon arrival Mary notices the stone is removed, and the body as well. The dead body of Jesus cannot be found—and with good reason. But for now Mary makes haste to inform Simon Peter and the Beloved Disciple. Peter and the Beloved race (more like compete!) to the tomb. After finding the tomb empty, each draws his own conclusion and returns home.

Mary of Magdala remains. It is usually left to the womenfolk to bury the dead and anoint the dearly departed with their tears. It is no different with Mary. Yet it is now the hour of the unexpected. Tears must cease and the eye of faith must clearly see *who* is at hand. A stranger raises a familiar question: "Whom are you looking for?" Not a query for the intellect, or a polite offer to be of assistance. One's whole life is thrown into question by the Questioner. Mary is looking for Jesus. Yet she is looking for him in all the wrong places.

The veil must be lifted. The tears must cease. Mary *turns* as the Gardener pronounces her name, "Mary." Name begets title, "Rabboni!" (Teacher.) Mary's faith is maturing as is her recognition of the One who is Stranger, Gardener, and now Teacher. There is another step in her journey. Mary is sent by Jesus to proclaim his message to the disciples. She does so. Mary testifies: "I have seen the Lord." The Teacher has become her *Lord*. The identity of Jesus is revealed and proclaimed. Such a recognition comes to Mary because she has been looking for the Lord all along. Mary went to the tomb to minister to the dead Jesus. She goes to the disciples and proclaims the risen Christ who has *found her*. For the Jesus who healed her is the same Lord who now calls her by name, and sends her forth to proclaim his resurrection.

Can this be the same Mary who long ago was possessed of evil spirits? Can this be the Mary who was judged to be of ill repute? Can this be the Mary who anointed Jesus' feet with ointment and tears and dried them with her hair?

Yes, this is the same Mary in terms of flesh and blood. *No*, this is a new Mary in terms of being born anew in the Spirit. The Pharisee Nicodemus wanted to know how one could be born again. His understanding of birth was purely biological and carnal. Jesus taught that there is a birth beyond the flesh, and a new life that comes through grace. This rebirth was a theological stumbling block and intellectual obscurity to Nicodemus. Yet to those born from above, being born again is to be recreated through the Spirit. Such is not a matter of loyalty, intellect, biology, or the laws of nature. To be reborn is a gift of grace and the loving work of the Spirit. The reality of rebirth is revealed in the lives of those who respond to Jesus' question—"Whom are you looking for?"—with "You, my Lord and God."

One such life is Mary of Magdala. She received a great gift, namely, a second chance. We all stumble on our pilgrimage of faith toward that City not made by human hands. We need to know that a fall is not fatal because we are extended a hand up by the One who extended himself downward into our flesh. God's unbounded love for creation, creatures great and small, is evidenced by our being given a second chance. Jesus comes not to condemn but to save.

Now all of this sounds quite abstract and bloodless. Hence, we look to the life of Mary of Magdala. She was possessed of evil spirits. She suffered a bad reputation in the town. In other words, she was a prime candidate for a second chance. And that is what Jesus did for her. He gave her back her life. He challenged her to take this second chance and live a new way. No mention is ever made of Mary *deserving* a second chance, for God's mercy is not conditioned by our merit. All is grace. All that is requested of us is that we open all our being to the Spirit. There is no mention of Jesus giving long moral sermons or writing detailed programs of ethics. Jesus gives himself in love to the one in need. This is enough. This is the amazing grace which saves us from the wretchedness of sin.

To some degree all of us suffer from our past. We have episodes which cause us to blush. We want the mountains to fall on us, the hills to cover our thoughts and deeds. The burden of sin and guilt can cut deep into our being. We can feel like Cain—our sins are too great to be forgiven. Mary of Magdala reminds us that our sins are too great *not* to be forgiven. We need the greater love offered by Jesus. When no one understands, there is One who knows us by name. There is One who has counted all the hairs on our head. There is One who searches our heart and still loves us. It is the same One who gave Mary her second chance.

We return to the Garden with Jesus and Mary. He tells her, "Do not hold on to me." She is sent to the disciples to tell the story of the risen Lord. Mary is sent to us as well. She tells us, "I have seen the Lord. The One who gave me back my life is risen."

What Jesus did for Mary, he will do for us. He will do for *you*.

23

Priscilla:
To Teach

The portraits in our gallery of women are dwindling down to a precious few. From the mother of us all to the Magdala who is the first witness to the risen Lord, the women painted by brush and pen are well known. Even those without names have acquired a familiarity through Sunday school and sermon: Lot's wife, the Samaritan woman at the well, and the mite of the poor widow have formed characters and inspired hearts. Before we conclude with the most famous of biblical women, Mary the mother of Jesus, we encounter a woman *with* a name who *lacks* recognition. She is Priscilla. And appropriately, she is a teacher. This woman without name recognition serves in a ministry often lacking recognition. It is the perfect fit of minister to ministry.

Teachers are often blessed, and burdened, with outstanding students. There is a spark in the eye which signals a flame in the brain for truth. There is a thirst for knowledge and a hunger for wisdom. Such a student possesses, and is possessed by, a spirit of curiosity which does not kill the cat but reveals the nine lives of creativity. These students are driven to look beyond the surface and beneath the obvious. They challenge teachers to revise notes and be renewed in spirit. The blessing of such students is that they require of teachers more than suitable textbooks. They demand *text-teachers*. Those who are privileged to teach do more than impart information and form the intellect. Text-teachers live the lesson and provide visibility to the most sublime of truths. Such teachers enlarge hearts, open minds, discipline wills, and strengthen moral character. The teacher blessed with an outstanding student returns the blessing by being an outstanding teacher. Blessing begets blessing.

In the Acts of the Apostles, a biblical history of the early church, we encounter an influential student and an outstanding teacher. The student is Apollos. The teacher is Priscilla.

109

From the text (Acts 18:23-28) we learn that Apollos is a Jew from Alexandria who traveled to Ephesus. Apollos is described as an "eloquent man" who is also "well versed in the Scriptures." Intellectually, Apollos had been a disciple of John, having received a baptism from him. This disciple of John is a man of the Holy Spirit and proclaims Jesus with truth and conviction. On one occasion Apollos is giving witness about Jesus in the synagogue. It so happens that Priscilla is present. She is impressed with his knowledge and sincerity. In fact, Priscilla was so taken with Apollos that "she took him and expounded to him the way of God more accurately."

This seemly ordinary episode is extraordinary in its profound simplicity. An influential, eloquent Jew is preaching in the synagogue—about Jesus! A woman hears Apollos's testimony and takes him aside to *teach him* "the way of God more accurately." The teachable moment, the time of profound truth and grace, is revealed: teachers able to see with insight the pupil-person before them, the gifted student with the humility essential for genuine learning. Priscilla is not intimidated or threatened by the position, eloquence, or intelligence of Apollos. Her focus is on Jesus and the opportunity to teach more deeply about the Lord. Apollos is wise enough to know that he knows not. He is a genuine seeker of truth who has the humility to learn from all who offer the gift of knowledge. There is no hint that Apollos felt demeaned by this woman's offer to instruct. The baptism of John is incomplete. This woman offers to mature that baptism into the Baptism of the Lord Jesus Christ.

Predictably, we are not told how the teaching and learning progressed—at least not directly. We are offered hints which indicate the outcome was fruitful: Apollos was accepted and encouraged by the local church, even to the extent of being recommended to the disciples. Apollos was no mere talker but "greatly helped those who through grace had believed." Furthermore, Apollos was able to give convincing public testimony that Jesus is the Christ, based on his knowledge of Scripture. Hence, the reviews are most favorable. So it seems.

A fundamental requirement of teaching: teachers remain in place, pupils move on. It is a grace to teach, influence, and form another person. Teaching is a relationship of ultimate trust which calls for the total commitment to the good of the student. There is an implied sadness in every teaching relationship. The pupils who come will also go. There can be no holding on. Teaching is to send forth. Teachers know the joy of giving birth to ideas and dreams. Teachers know the sadness of freeing students to flower in the soil of some distant shore. Teachers know the resurrection that comes with the student who returns to share the "hidden years." The mystic cords of memory that connect teacher and student endure in ways unseen. Yet there are moments when lessons learned long ago rush to the conscious mind with a power that inspires a letter, telephone call, or in-person appearance. The debt is repaid and the receiver of earlier gifts returns the gift: "The words you spoke that day didn't mean much. However, over the years I have come to see what you tried to tell me." All the frustrations, disappointments, and seeming failures evaporate. The denial of instant gratification and immediate victories only makes such moments more precious and rare.

Of course teachers know "the silent ones" with years and lives forever hidden. There are special corners of a teacher's mind reserved for these. Try as they might, teachers cannot forget the ones who seem to have forgotten them. Teachers search for bits of news, loose gossip, or some hearsay testimony about those students who have fallen off the radar screen. The Bermuda Triangle seems to have gobbled up their lives along with those traces of long ago. Teachers cannot help but wonder if the silence is due to some early hurt or later misfortune or wrong which leaves lingering resentment or painful embarrassment. Teachers long to heal the hurts and help with present problems.

Students often outdistance teachers in fame and fortune. So it is with Apollos and his teacher, Priscilla. Apollos's star is on the ascent. He is embarking on an influential ministry of preaching the Gospel. Apollos will even become a fellow worker of the Apostle Paul. Apollos, for example, has a very powerful influence on the Corinthian community. His learning, eloquence, and material abundance draw many to Jesus. Yet there is a danger. The minister is not greater than the message; nor does he stand above the Gospel. Apollos must always proclaim Jesus and not himself. Fidelity, not success, is the measure of the minister and ministry. There is always a danger that Apollos will come to value human praise more than the glory of God. Divisions can arise within a community over a popular preacher. Apollos, who "learned Christ" from Priscilla and Aquila, must continually "learn Christ" until the Lord calls him home.

And what about Priscilla? She remains in Ephesus. There are others to instruct fully in Christ Jesus. This teacher will not travel to distant lands. She will not know the public spotlight. The adulation of the crowd and the praise of a congregation will elude her. Yet her ministry is no less important or lasting. For in a way Priscilla does travel, preaching and teaching about Jesus Christ. She does so through the voices and lives of those she has touched and forever influenced. Apollos is able to influence so many because of the influence of his teacher at Ephesus.

We can easily picture the scene in the synagogue: a young man filled with zeal, preaching about Jesus. The crowd is captivated by his eloquence and the depth of his knowledge. Yet there is something missing. Priscilla can't help but think, "He sounds so much like Apollos. I wonder if . . ."

The story continues.

24

Mary, the Mother of Jesus:
Let It Be

Highly Favored

Into the ordinary of life and time and place,
the Messenger to Mary announces the Gift of grace.
The Eternal Word to assume a human face.

This Offspring of the Spirit
is born from above.
In His life and death revealed
that Love beyond love.

Oh Highly Favored, full of grace,
Mother to the Savior of
the human race,
Your "yes" of faith inspires those
of low degree.
You justly feed
the neglected
hungry.

Deeply Troubled

Highly Favored, Mary of grace,
Deeply Troubled Virgin,
the Word of Life now lives within.
The rhyme gives way to reason:
"How can this be?
The Eternal now temporal in me."

Be not afraid is the heavenly refrain.
The gain is more than worth the pain.
The Kingdom of Peace and Justice true,
will come with the birth
of this Child on earth.
And your deeply troubled heart
will find its way through
the dark.

What do you say, O Virgin, to the
message heard?
"Let it be according to the Word.
Let the Light shine ever bright,
into the fears of my night."

Greatly Loved

Messenger departs, there is much to ponder
within the heart.
The mystery is about to start,
for God's new work of Sacred Art.
For His Son now grows within
the one who said her "yes" to Him.
Birth comes with a cry and the shedding of blood;
early lessons of true love.
The cry in the Crib; cry from the Cross;
each one a Love that bespeaks a loss.
But Hope will not be driven away;
despair has not the final
word to say.
There is a dawn that scatters doom,
the rising Son who dispels
the gloom.
Victory by the Light of Life does not
come without a price.
Payment on this ragged hill
bespeaks those loving wills,
of she who said,
"Let it be";
the Son who prayed,
"Thy will be done through me."

Afterword:
A Portrait for Today

What is stranger than the familiar? What bespeaks grace more than the ordinary? What reveals the mysterious as much as the everyday? Consider the human face. *Your* face. It is at once well known, yet there are moments when its elusive identity fills the heart with anxiety. *Who* is this who who looks back at you?

> Bathroom mirror on the wall,
> time to brush and wash.
> *Who* is this of morning's call?
> Through eyes of sleep and dreams long past;
> I still to see
> if the image is me.
> Is it the same *Who* of morning's light,
> I now view in the night?
> Is the *Who* of brush and wash,
> the same *Who* of gargle, floss?
> Or, in the end, is the *Who*
> a game of let's pretend?
> Or, is the abiding ever hiding
> in the constantly changing?

The preceding pages of portraits and prose have admitted us into the company of extraordinary women. At the same time these companions for the journey are familiar. We have grown up with them. These "surrogate parents and significant others" have taught us about the lure of sin and the power of lust; the valor of Judith and the virtue of Susanna. The darker side of self is revealed in Jezebel and Delilah. The finer angels make their

115